T0359303

CORPORATE AND TRUST STRUCTURES

Legal and Illegal Dimensions

CORPORATE AND TRUST STRUCTURES

Legal and Illegal Dimensions

EDITED BY
DAVID CHAIKIN & GORDON HOOK

Australian Scholarly

First published 2018 by
Australian Scholarly Publishing Pty Ltd
7 Lt Lothian St Nth, North Melbourne, Vic 3051

Tel: 03 9329 6963 / Fax: 03 9329 5452
enquiry@scholarly.info / www.scholarly.info

ISBN 978-1-925588-86-6

Cover design Wayne Saunders

Contents

Preface

This collection of essays was inspired by a seminar organised at the University of Sydney Business School in late 2016 involving academics, practitioners, consultants and international experts who came together to discuss and explore the legitimate and illegitimate uses of company and trust structures. In the same year there were Australian government policy initiatives to change aspects of company law relating to beneficial ownership disclosure as well as media reports about unfair tax advantages relating to family trusts. On the international scene, the Panama Papers revelations naming high profile politicians, heads of state, CEOs of large companies, entertainers and sports organisations received intense media scrutiny shining a spotlight on offshore companies, trusts and tax havens. So intense was the media interest that some of the persons named in the revelations paid a high career price. [1]

The editors of this book became aware of the need to step back from the media stories and some reported misconceptions and to take stock of the economic and other benefits derived from company and trust structures but also to highlight more accurately some of the issues around illicit use and exploitation of those structures. Nine contributors, including the editors, each experts in their field, provided a forum for a number of participants from a variety of sectors – public, private, academia and media – to discuss issues ranging from basic concepts in company and trust law, E-commerce, entrepreneurship, the exploitation of companies and trusts for money laundering, law enforcement issues associated with the Panama Papers and new technologies. Subsequent to the seminar, and taking note of changes in the law and emerging issues, the authors expanded their contributions, refined their analyses and had their chapters independently reviewed. The final result is this book which should appeal to academics, practitioners and the general public including those coming to these topics for the first time.

Companies and trusts have long been part of the legal landscape of many countries. Both have advantages for business and personal purposes. Properly used they can achieve stability in business operations, provide management advantages and offer tax benefits. Companies encourage investment through limitation of liability for investors and in turn provide an engine for employment with obvious resulting social benefits. While not offering the same limited liability found with companies, trusts also provide excellent investment incentives as well as a platform to manage personal wealth, protection of family assets and estate planning. A trust arrangement is governed largely by the common law and rules of equity developed

---

1 The Prime Minister of Iceland (Sigmundur David Gunnlaugsson) resigned in 2016 in the wake of some of the information disclosed in the Panama Papers with which he was confronted by a BBC reporter.

as a body of law over centuries of judicial decision-making. Differing forms of trusts such as fixed trusts, discretionary trusts, testamentary trusts and those implied by the operation of law (such as constructive or resulting trusts) serve a variety of different purposes not all of which relate to business undertakings.

But companies and trusts also have attributes that make them attractive to criminals. Both companies and trusts create layers (in some countries impenetrable layers) between corporate entities and trusts, on the one hand, and beneficial owners, on the other. These impenetrable layers have been seen by criminals as a vulnerability easily exploited for tax evasion, money laundering and 'sanctions busting', and have turned some companies and trusts into contributing factors in destabilising economies, defeating international policy and perpetuating poverty.

The Panama Papers mentioned above involved the unauthorised disclosure of 11.5 million documents relating to hundreds of thousands of clients world-wide, spanning 40 years, from just one Panamanian law firm. The disclosures were eye-opening, for who was named, and shocking, in terms of the scale of hidden funds and assets through the use of multi-layered corporate and trust structures.[2] In a recent publication by the National Bureau of Economic Research it was estimated that the equivalent of 10 per cent of the global gross domestic product, or US$7.5 trillion, is held in offshore tax havens.[3] If this estimate is true (and there are estimates of much higher figures)[4] it is a staggering amount of wealth. Even if half that amount were available for taxation, the social and economic benefits would be enormous.

The chapters in this book collectively answer some key questions for both novices and experts, such as the legal nature of companies and trusts, the mechanisms developed to attribute corporate liability, the international legal requirements to mitigate the risk of criminal exploitation of companies and trusts and some of the law enforcement lessons learned from the Panama Papers revelations.

Chapter 1 looks at the concept of a trust in theory and in practice. The precise legal nature of a trust is outlined and shows that, in theory, it is a relationship between certain parties. In practice, however. a trust has been viewed, particularly in the United States as a kind of 'quasi-company' which involves contractual or other

---

2 See, Bastian Obermeyer and Frederick Obermaier, *The Panama Papers, Breaking the Story of How the Rich and Powerful Hide their Money* (Oneworld Publications Ltd, 2017). This book provides a fascinating account of the data leaks, to whom the leaks were made, the use of the information, and the scale of abuse of companies and trusts for illicit purposes, including tax evasion.

3 Annette Alstadsæter, Niels Johannesen, and Gabriel Zucman, *Who Owns The Wealth In Tax Havens? Macro Evidence And Implications For Global Inequality*, Working Paper 23805, Cambridge, Massachusetts, September 2017: < www.nber.org/papers/w23805>.

4 James Henry, from the Tax Justice Network, estimated in 2012 that the figure was between US$21 trillion and $32 trillion. See James Henry, *The Price of Off-Shore Revisited: New Estimates For Missing Global Private Wealth, Income, Inequality and Lost Taxes* Tax Justice Network, July 2012: < www.taxjustice.net>.

consensual arrangements for economic and business purposes.

Chapter 2 discusses how trust structures are an important vehicle for investment in Australia and examines the 2009 report *Australia as a Financial Centre-Building on our Strengths* and its recommendations. The chapter considers the idea of 'passporting' which offers a structure whereby funds licensed in one country can be marketed to investors in any other country.

Chapter 3 surveys the issues associated with business 'start-ups' and discusses what type of company structure should be considered by entrepreneurs when commencing a new business. The chapter sets out the legal and business issues faced by entrepreneurs in innovative businesses, as well as providing insights into how to deal with various risks arising in a complex business environment.

Chapter 4 looks at the legal concept of attribution in corporate law. It surveys the principles of attributing liability to corporations by virtue of the acts of natural persons and in doing so canvasses common law and statutory rules. It concludes that the law in Australia is fraught with difficulty and uncertainty, thereby making it difficult to ensure that corporations are fully accountable for conduct carried on in their interest.

Chapter 5 examines the law relating to when the benefit of corporate limited liability may be ignored by the courts – 'lifting' the corporate veil. The chapter reviews a number of established and recent cases where it is becoming evident that there are situations for the sake of 'rough justice between the parties' where a peek under the veil should be permitted. The chapter argues that the difficulty in piercing the corporate veil at common law is a sound policy and that it should be departed from only in exceptional circumstances, such as fraud.

Chapter 6 closely examines the complex ownership structure of the Alibaba Group, breaking down its *de jure* and *de facto* ownership. It looks at the 'variable interest entity' and identifies the legal risks of this type of corporate structure. The author explores options to enhance management accountability within this type of structure which usually includes multiple entities across a number of jurisdictions.

Chapter 7 outlines the requirements of the Financial Action Task Force for countries and individual financial and non-financial institutions to assess the risk of money laundering and terrorist financing posed by companies and trusts, and looks at how well countries are doing in complying with those obligations. It concludes that current levels of compliance are poor.

Chapter 8 summarises just how certain mechanisms within corporate structures and trust arrangements can, and have, been exploited by criminals to hide and launder criminal proceeds. It then summarises the requirements of the international standards on disclosure of ownership and control of companies and trusts, and it looks at the levels of compliance by countries with those obligations. Levels of compliance are noted to be low.

Chapter 9 fleshes out the lessons arising from the disclosures associated with the Panama Papers. It takes a close look at the data leaks, how the information was managed by the persons to whom the data was sent and the journalists who published the information associated with the leaks, and it canvasses some of the issues associated with the Financial Action Task Force recommendations applicable to trust and company service providers (TCSP).

Chapter 10 breaks down the concept of money laundering, the role of professionals such as lawyers in criminal activity involving companies and trusts, and highlights some recent case developments. It also contains a question and answer session between two authors on these issues.

Since the 2016 seminar, which formed the inspiration for this book, much has happened that touches on many of the issues outlined in the chapters of this book. On the money laundering front, the Attorney-General's Department has issued a consultation paper on regulation of TCSPs[5] which has received a number of key comments from the Law Council and the Financial Service Council.[6] A consultation paper has also been issued by the Australian Government's Treasury Department raising a series of issues concerning increased transparency of beneficial ownership of companies.[7] The submissions to Treasury indicate a range of views from those who support legislation creating a central public register of beneficial ownership of companies (modelled on the UK law) to those who question the costs and benefits of a public register.[8]

A major development in August 2017 was the filing, in the Federal Court of Australia by AUSTRAC, of a claim against the Commonwealth Bank of Australia (Bank) for breaches of the *Anti-Money Laundering and Counter-Terrorism Financing Act 2006* (Cth) (*AML/CTF Act)* alleging massive failures by the Bank to file threshold and suspicious transaction reports to AUSTRAC in relation to money laundering and terrorist financing. The allegations have attracted serious interest globally given the size and importance of the Bank in the region and globally, but have not yet been tested. There has been intense speculation as to the size of any civil penalties if the Bank were found to have breached the law. In November 2017 the Federal Court

---

5 Australian Attorney-General's Department, *Trust and company service providers: a model for regulation under Australia's anti-money laundering and counter-terrorism financing regime* Available at <https://www.ag.gov.au/Consultations/Documents/AML-CTF/trust-company-service-providers-model-for-regulation.pdf>.

6 Both available at <https://www.ag.gov.au/search/results.aspx?k=corporations%20law>.

7 Australian Treasury Department, *Increased transparency of beneficial ownership of companies*, March 2017. Available at <https://treasury.gov.au/consultation/increasing-transparency-of-the-beneficial-ownership-of-companies/>.

8 The submissions are also available at <https://treasury.gov.au/consultation/increasing-transparency-of-the-beneficial-ownership-of-companies/>.

issued an important judgment in *AUSTRAC v Tab Limited (No. 3)*[9] which set out the relevant principles for applying civil penalties to violations of the *AML/CTF Act*.

Finally, the publication of the Paradise Papers in late 2017 has shone another light on the offshore financial sector. The Paradise Papers are said to be the largest data leak in history, eclipsing the Panama Papers, in that it consists of 13.4 million documents sourced from a Bermuda-based law firm/TCSP, a Hong Kong-based TCSP and 19 government-run corporate registries in small tax havens. The Paradise papers appear at first glance to be different from the Panama papers in that the persons and companies identified may be more respectable and mainstream, including the Queen of England. The Paradise Papers have raised important questions as to the ethical use of tax havens, particularly concerning the role of tax avoidance.

The editors would like to thank Joanne Webb and Roland Giddings for assisting in the organisation of the annual Discipline of Business Law conference, and Katherine Jolley for reading the manuscript and improving the language of the text. That gainsaid, the editors take full responsibility for any errors and omissions in the final manuscript.

Dr David Chaikin
Chair, Discipline of Business Law
University of Sydney Business School

Dr Gordon Hook
Executive Secretary
Asia/Pacific Group on Money Laundering

---

9 See *Chief Executive Officer of Australian Transaction Reports Analysis Centre v Tab Limited (No. 3)* [2017] FCA 1296 (10 November 2017). A $45 million civil penalty was imposed on Tabcorp as part of a settlement.

Chapter 1

The Tension Between a Concept of the Express Trust in Theory and Modern Commercial Practice

Derwent Coshott

When speaking of the concept of an express trust in theory and the ideas concerning trusts in modern commercial practice, we are not discussing unified conceptualisations but rather separate and possibly incompatible concepts. There is considerable disjunction between a theoretical conceptualisation of the express trust based on a doctrinal analysis, and the way that trusts are utilised in modern practice: between a rationalisation of trust law based on doctrine, and the way trusts are actually used by people today; including the reasons why they are used. The tension between these two – theory and practice – is, unsurprisingly, the driving force behind many current trust law developments, and is therefore, an area ripe for discussion.

The Concept of a Trust in Theory

At a doctrinal level, the express trust simply represents a series of default and mandatory rules that govern the creation and maintenance of a set of rights and obligations regarding legal and/or equitable rights held by one person (a trustee) on certain terms for another (a beneficiary, or the public in a charitable trust). Further, the express trust is not something that arose through considered forethought and design. The law of trusts developed over centuries through the decisions of individual chancellors and later judges settling real disputes that came before them. In the words of Heydon and Leeming, the law of trusts simply represents 'legal rules [that] are abstracted from the perceived effect of decided cases'.[1] As such, the express trust represents no more, and no less, than a collection of ad hoc rules, which grew out of decisions that are collected under the rubric of 'the law of trusts'.

Nevertheless, the law of trusts, while representing an ad hoc collection of rules, does not necessarily represent a random collection of them. There is a coherence, which is demonstrated by such efforts of abstraction Heydon and Leeming mention that reveal what the express trust is at its core: a legal relationship concerning

---

1 J.D. Heydon and M.J Leeming, *Jacob's Law of Trusts in Australia* (LexisNexis Butterworths, 8th edn., 2016) at [1–03].

property[2] held for the benefit of another; and it is this beneficial motivation that provides the underlying coherence for the rules which govern the relationship we recognise as an express trust. To understand how it is necessary to briefly outline these two essential features of the trust: firstly as a legal relationship; and secondly, as a relationship that exists for the benefit of another.

The Express Trust is a Legal Relationship

The express trust is, first and foremost, a relationship. Historically, a beneficiary's rights under an express trust were not in rem, i.e. proprietary, but rather in personam. Indeed, it was not until the late 17th century that a beneficiary's interest in an express trust came to be regarded as one in the trust property itself, and even then only with respect to what we would consider fixed trusts; not discretionary trusts.[3] This is because a beneficiary under a discretionary trust does not have anything recognised as proprietary, merely an interest contingent on a discretion being exercised in the beneficiary's favour;[4] while in a charitable trust, the subject matter of the trust is directed towards a valid purpose for the benefit of the public.[5]

Yet regardless of whether we are considering a charitable trust, or if a beneficiary's interest is fixed or not, every type of traditional express trust continues to be predicated on a personal relationship, in the sense that one cannot hold property on trust solely for oneself. The rights of beneficiaries, or the public, and the obligations of trustees are co-dependent and correlative: they cannot exist without the presence of another. This means, even in a private trust, a beneficiary's interest cannot be considered purely proprietary, or in rem. A beneficiary with a fixed interest in an express trust does not have direct unfettered rights to the trust property simply by virtue of being the object of a trust. This is because it is the terms of the trust itself that will determine the extent of a beneficiary's rights to the trust property; with many of those rights being defined by the obligations the trust imposes on

---

2 Note, that rights not considered as proprietary (such as certain contractual rights) can be held on trust. When done so, however, they are referred to as trust property, and it is in that sense the term 'property' is used here.

3 J.H. Baker, *An Introduction to English Legal History* (Oxford University Press, 4th edn., 2007) at 309–11.

4 *Hartigan Nominees Pty Ltd v Rydge* (1992) 29 NSWLR 405 at 443. Note however, it is possible to conceptualise a beneficiary's interest in the trust as proprietary through the concept of the fund (Richard Nolan, 'Property in a Fund' (2004) 120 *LQR* 108); and if all the beneficiaries are *sui juris* and absolutely entitled to the trust property, then under the rule in *Saunders v Vautrier* (1841) 41 ER 482 they may bring the trust to an end. Yet, as is explained below, the beneficiaries' rights to the trust are more about the obligations of the trustee in respect of the management of the property, and this is especially the case with respect to a beneficiary of a discretionary trust who may never derive any actual benefit from the trust.

5 Heydon and Leeming, above n1 at [1–07].

the trustee. Indeed, a beneficiary's interest in an express trust is always mediated through the trustee.

Two examples serve to illustrate the inherently bilateral nature of the trust relationship. The first regards a beneficiary's rights with respect to information regarding the trust property. Even considering a beneficiary with a fixed interest in the trust, which as noted has often been regarded as proprietary,[6] that beneficiary's right to information regarding the trust may be heavily modified by the terms of the trust, i.e. the obligations with respect to the information that is owed to the beneficiary.[7] The second example is the beneficiary's right to trace trust property.[8] A beneficiary has no direct right or control over trust property, which is why, even where a breach of trust gives rise to a tracing remedy, the property concerned is always restored to the trust, not to the beneficiary directly.[9] Only through the operation of the rule in Saunders v Vautier[10] can the trust property be directly transferred to the beneficiary, and the way this does so is by bringing the express trust to an end,[11] which naturally implies that while the trust exists there is no such direct right to the trust property.[12]

To Benefit Another

An express trust however cannot simply be understood as just a relationship concerning property. The reason is because the overarching purpose of this relationship is to benefit another: to benefit the beneficiary (in a private trust) or the

---

6 This derives from that beneficiary's interest being fixed and certain, although this basis has been queried by several leading decisions: *Re Londonderry's Settlement* [1965] Ch 918 at 932 and 938; *Hartigan Nominees Pty Ltd v Rydge* (1992) 29 NSWLR 405; *Schmidt v Rosewood Trust Ltd* [2003] 2 AC 709. Note a further argument is that the right to information is based on a fiduciary obligation: *Morris v Morris* (1993) 9 WAR 150; *Breen v Williams* (1996) 186 CLR 71 at 89.

7 *Re Londonderry's Settlement* [1965] Ch 918 at 936–7; *Breakspear v Ackland* [2009] Ch 32 at 53; *SAS Trustee Corporation v Cox* [2011] NSWCA 408 at [148].

8 Which is often said to give rise to an *in rem* right to the property concerned, J.D. Heydon, M.J. Leeming and P.G. Turner, *Meagher, Gummow & Lehane's Equity: Doctrines & Remedies* (LexisNexis Butterworths, 5th edn., 2015) at [4–110].

9 John H Langbein, 'The Contractarian Basis of the Law of Trusts' (1995) 105 *Yale L.J.* 625 at 647–8.

10 (1841) 49 ER 282. The rule provides that where the beneficiaries are identified and of adult age, they may terminate an express trust and have the trustee's title to trust property transferred to them.

11 This is described by M.W. Lau, *The Economic Structure of Trusts: Towards a Property-based Approach* (Oxford University Press, 2011) 170, as an, 'exit strategy'; or a means of 'ridding beneficiaries of the trustee's shackles'.

12 Of course, the rule in *Saunders v Vautier* has no role to play in charitable trusts.

public (in a charitable trust).[13]

The concept of benefiting another is at the core of what defines an express trust. In the private trust context, for example, to benefit the beneficiary recognises that the trust is a relationship for the beneficiary, and no one else. It gives content to the view expressed in the US that the trust is, 'a gift, projected on the plane of time and so subjected to a management regime.'[14] That is why benefiting the beneficiary is explicitly referred to as an overarching concept that goes to the validity of an express trust. As Millet LJ stated in *Armitage v Nurse:*[15]

> … there is an irreducible core of obligations owed by the trustees to the beneficiaries and enforceable by them which is fundamental to the concept of a trust. If the beneficiaries have no rights enforceable against the trustees there are no trusts.[16]

This 'irreducible core' represents a mandatory minimum obligation by trustees, 'to perform the trusts honestly and in good faith for the benefit of the beneficiaries'.[17] Buss JA, citing, inter alia, *Armitage v Nurse,* in *Scaffidi v Montevento Holdings* also stated,

> The office [of trustee] exists for the benefit of the beneficiaries: *Letterstedt v Broers* (1884) 9 App Cas 371, 386. It is an essential element of the trust that the trustee is under a personal obligation to deal with the trust property for the benefit of the beneficiaries, an obligation giving correlative rights to the beneficiaries.[18]

This is mirrored in the United States, where the benefit-the-beneficiaries standard has been given equal, if not greater, emphasis than in England and Australia through the *Restatement (Third) of Trusts* and the *Uniform Trust Code.* Here it is explicitly featured as an overarching requirement of trust law to which all other trust rules are subject, and against which the terms of any express trust are tested.[19]

---

13 Likewise, in the charitable context the same motivations are evident. As Heydon and Leeming, above n1 at [1–07], write, in a charitable trust, 'there will be no individuals as beneficiaries. There, the beneficiary must be regarded as the charitable purpose to which the trust property is devoted.'

14 John H Langbein, 'Mandatory Rules in the Law of Trusts' (2004) 98 *Nw. U. L. Rev.* 1105 at 1109, citing Bernard Rudden, 'Review, John P. Dawson, Gifts and Promises' (1981) 44 *Mod. L. Rev.* 610.

15 [1998] Ch 241.

16 Id at 253.

17 Ibid.

18 [2011] WASCA 14 at [149].

19 Langbein, above n14 at 1106. Langbein, at 1108–9, also goes on to note that this standard is equally applicable to charitable trusts: 'In the realm of charitable trusts, the ancient

The benefit-the-beneficiaries standard extends further into the various rules of express trusts however than simply regulating the extent to which trustee obligations may be excluded or modified. One salient example in the context of private trusts is the rule against perpetuities, which is often stated to exist in order to ensure that property is not tied up in trusts indefinitely.[20] This is not entirely correct however, and militates in favour of the need to understand the law of trusts as a set of rules that developed incrementally, by analogy, and therefore with a degree of doctrinal cohesion. Thus the operation of the rule against perpetuities is related to the rule against restraints on alienation in the law of property generally, and the rule against indestructible trusts. The rule against restraints on alienability holds that if a person has received property absolutely, then an attached condition purporting to completely restrict that person dealing with the property will be void.[21] The rule against indestructible trusts holds that a trust's terms cannot prevent the beneficiary from using and eventually exhausting the trust;[22] or, bringing it to an end under the rule in *Saunders v Vautier*.[23] Naturally, if a trust does not vest in a beneficiary

---

charitable purpose doctrine serves a function comparable to the benefit-the-beneficiaries standard by requiring any purported charitable trust to satisfy standards of public benefit. Under the charitable purpose doctrine, a charitable trust must serve purposes 'of such social interest or benefit to the community' that the trust merits the 'special privileges that are typically allowed to charitable trusts,' most notably, exemption from the rule against perpetuities. The courts police the requirement of charitable benefit by insisting on objective criteria for determining what constitutes public benefit, as well as by applying an anti-inurement rule forbidding the use of charitable-trust assets for private gain.'

20 The rule against perpetuities requires that, where an interest in an express trust will not vest in a beneficiary until sometime after the trust is constituted, that interest must vest within the lifetime of a life or lives in being at the constitution of the trust plus 21 years. While it is a rule of property law generally, it takes on particular significance in the trust context, and thus if the terms of the trust demonstrate the rule will be violated, the trust will fail. In order for the interest to be considered as vested, the beneficiaries must be known, as must their respective interests. This means where the terms of the trust indicate that even one member of the class will not take until after the perpetuity period, the trust will be void. Statutory reform however, has significantly altered the operation of the rule in many jurisdictions, if not outright abolished it in others, e.g. South Australia; Pennsylvania and New Jersey in the US. In Australia, those reforms where the rule has been modified can generally be said to have had three effects. The first is specifying the vesting period in an amount of years (80 years in the majority of Australian jurisdictions). The second is adopting various rules that require the court to wait and see if an interest will vest outside the perpetuity period. The third is if the vesting period is exceeded, to allow the court to vary the vesting date of the interest and/or exclude beneficiaries from the class of objects in order to preserve the validity of the trust.

21 *Hall v Busst* (1960) 104 CLR 206; *Nullagine Investments Pty Ltd v Western Australian Club Inc* (1993) 177 CLR 635 at 649–50.

22 *Brandon v Robinson* (1811) 34 ER 379; *Re Cain* [1950] VR 382 at 391.

23 (1841) 49 ER 282.

or imposes complete restraints on alienability then it will be indestructible. The coextensive nature of these rules is recognised in South Australia, which despite famously abolishing the rule against perpetuities[24] preserves, through the presence of express statutory provisions, the rule in *Saunders v Vautier*[25] and grants the court powers to order the vesting of interests.[26]

If a trust is for the benefit of the beneficiaries, then the purpose underlying the rule against perpetuities is to ensure those beneficiaries actually benefit. Doctrinally speaking, the express trust is a transfer of the benefit of legal and/or equitable rights to another. In this context, the reason why the rule against perpetuities exists is to prevent settlors from being able to control property indefinitely via the terms of the trust; hence the term, restraining the settlor's dead-hand.[27] If the settlor has no rights of enforcement with respect to the trust, given the settlor has parted with the benefit of the legal and/or equitable rights subject to it, then it does not make sense that the terms of the trust should allow the settlor's continued interference via another means. That being said there is an obvious policy in the law that, while indefinite and absolute interference is unacceptable, temporary and partial interference is acceptable. The rule against perpetuities therefore ensures that a balance is kept between the competing interests of the settlor, in establishing the trust, and the beneficiaries, by essentially referring the settlor's intention to the overarching purpose of the trust: to benefit the beneficiaries, which is taken to be the settlor's overarching objective intention in establishing the trust to begin with.

The Concept of the Trust in Practice

As shown, on a doctrinal level the express trust is a collection of largely coherent rules that regulate and give meaning to the concept of the trust as a legal relationship regarding legal and/or equitable rights managed for the benefit of a beneficiary. In practice however, the trust has moved in different directions.

In the asset protection sphere, the development of the non-charitable purpose trust was not driven by the desire to benefit another, but quite the opposite. In this context the trust structure has been adopted thanks to the division between actual and beneficial ownership provided by the trust structure. As noted above, in a traditional charitable purpose trust, the beneficiary has been called the charitable purpose itself,[28] but it is also the benefit to the public, or more accurately, a section thereof that gives charitable purpose trusts their validity.[29] Farcically, non-charitable

---

24 *Law of Property Act 1936* (SA), s 61.

25 Ibid s 62A.

26 Ibid s 62.

27 Langbein, above n14 at 1107–19.

28 Heydon and Leeming, above n1 at [1–07].

29 *Helena Partnerships Ltd v Commissioner for Her Majesty's Revenue and Customs* [2012]

purpose trusts established in 'offshore' jurisdictions eschew both requirements. For example, the STAR trust established by the Cayman Islands in 1997 allows trust property to be held on trust for the purposes of a transaction.[30] In substance however there is a beneficiary in the sense that someone does economically benefit from the transaction; but by structuring an express trust in this way it ensures that neither the trustee, nor the person who actually benefits from the trust, is treated as the beneficial owner of the trust property.

In the more mundane context of traditional common law trust jurisdictions, the express trust is, in practice, often employed to function as a kind of quasi-company. Again, this is not done for reasons that have anything to do with the doctrinal foundations of trust law. Rather it is to take advantage of the more flexible management regime of a trust as opposed to a registered company, while retaining a level of insolvency protection for beneficial owners. In Australia, this is achieved through a combination of trust-drafting and extra-contractual arrangements; what D'Angelo terms 'contractualisation' which is an,

> … idea involving the use of private bargaining techniques, and contractual and contract-like documentary evidence derived from and operating in a manner analogous to contractual principles, to shape or reallocate the risks of any of the … principal participants in the commercial trust enterprise.[31]

Such contractualisation processes include what are termed 'special contracts', which represent contracts between the parties to the trust that 'may have the effect of expanding or limiting the obligations, duties or liabilities' otherwise created by terms of the trust.[32] The result is an arrangement where the 'regulation and enforcement' of the fiduciary relationship 'is influenced by a combination of contract and fiduciary law.'[33] The final product is an economic, if not legal, entity that is governed by a combination of contractual arrangements and trust law: the express trust itself is simply the core of a broader legal web of consensual arrangements.

In the United States, Delaware has taken the logic of such thinking to its

---

EWCA Civ 569 at [78] (Lloyd J). *Re Income Tax Acts (No 1)* [1930] VLR 211 at 222–3 (Lowe J); *Re Compton; Powell v Compton* [1945] Ch 123 at 131 (Lord Greene MR); *Oppenheim v Tobacco Securities Co Ltd* [1951] AC 297 at 306 (Lord Simonds).

30 *Special Trusts (Alternative Regime) Law 1997*, later consolidated in the *Trusts Law (2001 Revision)*. See also, Alec R Anderson, 'Statutory Non-Charitable Purpose Trust: Estate Planning in the Tax Havens' in D.W.M. Waters (ed.) *Equity, Fiduciaries and Trusts* (Carswell, 1993) at 99.

31 Nuncio D'Angelo, *Commercial Trusts* (LexisNexis Butterworths, 2014) [1.52].

32 Id at [2.129]; *Alpha Wealth Financial Services Pty Ltd v Frankland River Olive Company Ltd* [2008] WASCA 119 at [89] (Buss JA).

33 D'Angelo, above n31 at [2.135]; Paul D. Finn, 'Contract and the Fiduciary Principle' (1989) 12 *UNSWLJ* 76; Paul D. Finn, 'Fiduciary Reflections' (2014) 88 *ALJ* 27.

ultimate conclusion through the legislative establishment of the statutory business trust, which is in substance a corporation whose governance structure is almost entirely default law.[34] As such, the statutory business trust provides the protection of full limited liability,[35] in addition to having its own legal identity[36] and perpetual existence.[37] Essentially, the statutory business trust is a company emptied of almost any mandatory requirements, and is, in the words of Hansmann, Kraakman and Squire, 'the final step in the historical evolution of commercial entities.'[38] That is because it provides what many scholars argue the express trust should do: to serve as a 'nexus of contracts'; 'a collection of business relationships organised within a legal framework; a kind of coordinative hub for various legal persons to enter into contractual relationships with one another for their mutual economic benefit.'[39] As the *Delaware Statutory Trust Act* explicitly states its policy is, 'to give maximum effect to the principle of freedom of contract and to the enforceability of governing instruments.'[40] The development of such a trust structure is therefore directly influenced by the perceived commercial desires of people who would seek such an efficient, more cost-effective, legal structure than provided by corporations through which to run their enterprises, while granting them the flexibility that is traditionally associated with the trust framework and the protections of limited liability.

The question may be asked though, to what extent are the interests of the trust's beneficiaries/shareholders protected, other than through the entity/owner shielding this particular legal structure was created to provide? The argument that is adopted by law and economics scholars is a fundamentally neoclassical economics rationale: that the users of such entities are, as rational economic actors, the best capable to decide for themselves the nature of their legal relationship.[41] Therefore, whatever

34 Robert Sitkoff, 'An Agency Costs Theory of Trust Law' (2004) 89 *Cornell L. Rev.* 621 at 681; Henry Hansmann, 'Corporation and Contract' (2006) 8 *American Law and Economics Review* 1, at 3; Henry Hansmann and Reinier Kraakman, 'The Essential Role of Organizational Law' (2000) 110 *Yale L.J.* 387 at 432.

35 § 3805.

36 § 3810(a)(2).

37 § 3808(a).

38 Henry Hansmann, Reinier Kraakman and Richard Squire, 'Law and the Rise of the Firm' (2006) 119 *Harv. L. Rev.* 1333 at 1397.

39 Harold Demsetz, 'The Theory of the Firm Revisited' (1988) 4(1) *Journal of Law, Economics & Organization* 141 at 154–6; Michael C. Jensen and William H. Meckling, 'Theory of the Firm: Managerial Behavior, Agency Costs and Ownership Structure' (1976) 3 *J. Fin. Econ.* 305 at 310; Lau, above n11 at 37–42; Henry Hansmann and Ugo Mattei, 'The Functions of Trust Law: A Comparative and Legal Analysis' (1998) 73 *New York University Law Journal* 434 at 470.

40 § 3825(b).

41 J. Persky, 'Retrospectives: The Ethology of Homo Economicus' (1995) 9(2), *The Journal of Economic Perspectives* 221; R.A. Posner, *Economic Analysis of Law* (Wolters Kluwer, 8th

they chose is to their benefit, even if from a doctrinal legal perspective that would not appear to be the case. This however is not the same thing as a legal relationship established for the benefit of another; and the question may legitimately be asked whether, when considering such developments as statutory business trusts and non-charitable purpose trusts, we are looking at a trust in name only.

Conclusion

The concept of a trust in theory is one based around the notion that a trust is a legal relationship for another's benefit. Yet that is not reflected in these examples of its practice. This is why there have been calls for the reform of the 'commercial trust' which denotes the use of an express trust structure in a commercial context, i.e. one where the trust structure is not employed in pursuance of its traditional, doctrinal purpose.[42] There is nothing inherently incorrect in such efforts. They seek to create a legal structure that is attractive to investors, and so will encourage a greater share of international investment in Australia.[43] It is essential however to understand the core of a trust when speaking of modifying the law of trusts, or adapting the trust structure for particular uses. If we ignore the way the various rules of trusts are dependent on one another, together with their motivating principles, we risk losing sight of what the trust is, and what it means. This confusion is already becoming evident through the plethora of theories of the trust comparing it to corporations[44] and/or contracts,[45] which are based on its developing practical uses as opposed to its doctrinal core. We must therefore be cautious of conflating the doctrinal concept of an express trust with a concept based on how it is being utilised in practice, and be ever mindful of both when seeking to understand and further develop the law of trusts.

---

edn., 2011) 3; D'Angelo, above n31 at [1.65].

42 D'Angelo, above n31 at [1.31].

43 David Chaikin and Eve Brown, 'Global Competitiveness and Exporting Financial Services: A proposal for an Alternative Australian Trusts Act' (University of Sydney Business School and the Financial Services Council, 2015) at [2.1]: <http://www.fsc.org.au/downloads/file/policy/AATA_final.pdf>.

44 Hansmann and Mattei, above n39.

45 Langbein, above n9.

Chapter 2

Trusts, Collective Investment and Passporting Australia's Capability

Carla Hoorweg

Trusts underpin the investment market in Australia. Since the 1930s, Australian investors have exclusively used trusts as the mechanism to pool money and invest for a common purpose. Whether investment is made through a professionally managed fund or a compulsory superannuation account, a trust is always the underlying vehicle.

Australia has considerable experience managing these trust-based investments. The growth of the compulsory superannuation system has resulted in the third largest pool of pension assets in the world[1] and these assets are managed predominantly by Australian managers. A unique pool of talent has developed in Australia consisting of investment experts with an ecosystem of support services around them. Economists describe this scenario as a comparative advantage and it would follow that Australia should be a world-leading financial centre. Yet it isn't. Despite Australians managing $2.8 trillion of funds, only around 3.7 per cent ($104 billion) is sourced from offshore.[2] Compared to the United Kingdom, which sources 30 per cent from offshore, Hong Kong which sources 65 per cent, and Singapore which sources 80 per cent[3] Australia is doing poorly.

Why then is the number coming from offshore so low? Economic theory suggests that barriers must exist, barriers which are preventing capital from flowing to Australian managers.

Are trusts to blame?

In 2008, the Australian Financial Centre Forum was asked to report to the Government on how Australia could improve its competitiveness as a financial

---

1 Edmund Tang, *Australia Has the Third Largest Pension Fund Assets in the World,* Austrade Benchmark Report (6 July 2016): <https://www.austrade.gov.au/news/economic-analysis/australia-has-the-third-largest-pension-fund-assets-in-the-world>.

2 Australian Bureau of Statistics *5655.0, Managed Funds, Australia, Mar 2017*: <http://www.abs.gov.au/AUSSTATS/abs@.nsf/DetailsPage/5655.0Mar%202017?OpenDocument> at 1 August 2017, Table 9.

3 Sally Loane, 'Investment manager regime tax fixes a good start' *Investment Magazine (*24 July 2017): <https://investmentmagazine.com.au/2017/07/investment-manager-regime-tax-fixes-a-good-start/>.

services centre. In 2009 the Taskforce's report *Australia as a Financial Centre-Building on our Strengths* was delivered to government.[4] The Taskforce's Report became known as the *Johnson Report* after its Chair, former Deputy Chairman of Macquarie Bank, Mark Johnson. Australia's funds management capabilities were addressed in the findings:

> In the Forum's view, the funds management sector represents the leading example of a sector where Australia has a comparative advantage that could be better exploited, and where some sensible policy initiatives could significantly improve the scope for greater internationalisation of the sector.[5]

The *Johnson Report* concluded that Australia had developed a significant skill base in investment management with Australia having 'one of the largest and most sophisticated funds management sectors globally'.[6] The report concluded that this expertise had developed as a direct result of the Australian superannuation system, which now requires the management of around \$2.1 trillion in superannuation savings.[7] Australia was, however, considered to be punching below its weight when compared to London, Singapore and Hong Kong on the number of these services it provides to offshore clients.

The *Johnson Report* made a number of policy recommendations designed to increase the amount of funds-management export revenue. These included a broader range of collective investment vehicles than just the existing trust structure, development of regional architecture to ensure investment products could be more easily sold between jurisdictions and a number of technical tax improvements to ensure more appropriate outcomes for foreign investors.[8]

But why bother?

Improving Australia's competitiveness in this area could result in significant benefits to the economy over the medium term. In the case of funds' management, money sourced from offshore clients and managed by Australian fund managers is considered an export for trade purposes, despite no physical goods or services leaving Australian shores.

Investment money is highly mobile. The more attractive it is to either locate a fund in Australia, or use an Australian fund manager, the more jobs are created

---

4 Australian Financial Centre Forum, *Australia as a Financial Centre – Building on our Strengths* (November 2009) at 117: <http://cache.treasury.gov.au/treasury/afcf/content/final_report/downloads/AFCF_Building_on_Our_Strengths_Report.pdf>.

5 Id at 28.

6 Id at 11.

7 Australian Bureau of Statistics, above n2, Table 6.

8 Johnson Report, above n4 at 117–21.

here. A fund manager looking to set up an investment fund has the ability to choose any jurisdiction in the world in which to locate the fund (its domicile). The domicile does not have to be the same as the location of the underlying assets that the fund invests in. Nor does the fund have to be domiciled in the same location as the investors forming the fund's target market. However, the ancillary activities required to support an investment fund, such as administration, legal, registry and custody services, are usually located in the same jurisdiction in which the fund is domiciled, either to satisfy regulatory requirements or for efficiency reasons.

Research by Deloitte Access Economics shows that foreign fund flows contributed $434 million in total value to the Australian economy in 2012–13 and that a doubling of annual funds-management export revenue could result in an increase in GDP of approximately $330 million per annum by 2029–30.[9] Currently the proportion of funds sourced from overseas represents only 3.5 per cent of the total $2.8 trillion invested into Australian managed-investment schemes.[10]

There is bipartisan political support to grow the number of foreign-sourced funds. The *Johnson Report* set out the blueprint for Government to achieve this outcome. Many recommendations were accepted by the former Labor government at the time of the report[11] and the Coalition government has subsequently indicated its intention to progress the reforms.[12] A number of tax changes have already been initiated, release of the regulatory structure for a corporate collective investment is imminent and the Asia Region Funds Passport is due to commence from 1 January 2018.[13]

Trusts as investment funds – the regulatory & tax regimes

Since their introduction in 1998,[14] unitised, publicly offered managed-investment schemes have become embedded as the sole investment structure in Australia. At

---

9 Deloitte Access Economics, 'The economic impact of increasing Australian funds management exports' (Report prepared for the Financial Services Council, May 2014): <http://www.fsc.org.au/downloads/file/ResearchReportsFile/2014_0806_EconomicimpactofincreasingAustralianfundsmanagementexports_e64a.pdf>.

10 Australian Bureau of Statistics, above n2, Table 9.

11 Chris Bowen, 'Government response to Australia as a Financial Services Centre Report' (Press Release, 11 May 2010): <http://ministers.treasury.gov.au/DisplayDocs.aspx?doc=-pressreleases/2010/050.htm&pageID=&min=ceba&Year=&DocType=0>.

12 Kelly O'Dwyer, 'Address to the Financial Services Council Leaders' Summit, International Convention Centre, Sydney' (Speech delivered at the Financial Services Council Leaders' Summit, Sydney, 26 July 2017): <http://kmo.ministers.treasury.gov.au/speech/015-2017/>.

13 APEC website *Asia Region Funds Passport's Memorandum of Co-operation Comes Into Effect*: <http://fundspassport.apec.org/2016/06/30/asia-region-funds-passports-memorandum-of-co-operation-comes-into-effect/>.

14 *Managed Investments Act 1998* (Cth).

last count there are over 3,619 registered managed-investment schemes in Australia, operated by more than 593 licensed responsible entities.[15] Whilst the number of unregistered schemes is currently unknown, it is likely to be in the vicinity of the number of registered schemes, if not more.[16]

When used as collective investment vehicles, Australia's trust structures are subject to a number of layers of regulation. Those trusts satisfying the definition of a 'Managed Investment Scheme' are considered a financial product and subject to the financial services provisions of the *Corporations Act 2001* (Cth) and regulated by the Australian Securities and Investments Commission (ASIC). In addition to the fiduciary obligation that all trustees are under to their beneficiaries, the *Corporations Act* imposes a strict regulatory framework.

Trusts also satisfying the tax law definition of a 'Managed Investment Trust' receive certain concessional tax treatments to ensure investor outcomes are appropriate. This is essential to the effectiveness of the trust as a vehicle. Trust offer flow-through of taxation and do not charge tax themselves, unlike a company which is taxed at the corporate tax rate (currently 30 per cent). Instead the beneficiary receives pure income that has not been taxed and pays tax at their marginal tax rate. In the case of foreign investors, they receive a reduced withholding tax rate on any distributions they receive.

Determination of taxation outcomes for investment trusts is complex and requires navigating the intersection of the trust deed, equitable principles of trust law, taxation law, and corporations' law and requires carefully constructed policy settings to ensure investors do not face inconsistent taxation law outcomes.

History of trust taxation

Originally trusts were taxed under state legislation[17] until the imposition of Commonwealth income tax in 1915 through the *Income Tax Assessment Act 1915* (Cth). The uncertainty of trust taxation was apparent even before the Commonwealth legislation was introduced. State-based taxation laws were unclear as to which party bore the tax liability, correct treatment of accumulated income, and which taxation rate applied.[18] The new Commonwealth legislation alleviated some of this uncertainty. However, despite several amendments after its introduction, judicial

---

15 Australia Securities and Investments Commission (2016), *Annual Report.*

16 This is due to the common use of a wholesale/retail feeder structure, with many responsible entities using structures where the retail (registered) scheme invests into a wholesale (unregistered) scheme.

17 See eg *Land and Income Tax Assessment Act 1895* (NSW) and the equivalent legislation in Victoria.

18 Anthony Slater, 'Taxing trust income after Bamford's case' (2011) 40 *Australian Tax Review* 69 at 70.

interpretation continued to result in confusion, particularly regarding the issue of 'present entitlement'.[19] The *Income Tax Assessment Act 1936* (Cth) (ITAA 1936) was enacted with the intention of removing this confusion.

Historical information regarding the use of trusts as unitised collective investment vehicles in Australia is difficult to uncover. It is apparent that at least one such vehicle was on offer as early as 1938.[20] However there is little information about how prevalent their use was at this time. Across the shores 'public offer unit trusts' first emerged in England during the late 1860s and were provided as an alternative to limited liability companies, following a series of corporate collapses.[21] They fell out of favour for a number of years and re-emerged in the 1930s utilising a separate trustee and manager.[22] It is therefore likely that the popularity of unit trusts in Australia followed similar timing and that their prevalence did not increase, at least, until the late 1930s.

This historical context is important in understanding the manner in which trusts are taxed. When ITAA 1936 was enacted, trusts were predominantly closely held, testamentary or discretionary in nature[23] and collective investment schemes were in their infancy. The collective investment vehicles available for investment in today's market are the highly sophisticated, complex, commercially run descendants of the unit trusts of the 1930s.

The taxation law has recently been amended to modernise the treatment of trusts and to recognise their prevalent use as an investment structure in Australia. The Attribution Management Investment Trust taxation regime was implemented to improve the taxation of managed investment trusts and provide greater certainty for investors utilising these vehicles.[24] A key element of the regime is that it provides clarity for widely held investment trusts: that they will not be subject to the same rules as private or family trusts.

Whilst not specifically a recommendation of the *Johnson Report* (development of

---

19 Ibid.

20 Despite best efforts including a review of cases through the LexisNexis 'Casebase' service, the earliest record of an Australia unit trust that could be identified was the First Australian Unit Trust reporting its distribution for the year ended May 1938, see 'First Australian Unit Trust', *Brisbane Courier Mail* (17 June 1938) at 18: <http://trove.nla.gov.au/ndp/del/article/41002930>.

21 John Tarrant, 'Unit trusts in the 21st century' (2006) 20(3) *Commercial Law Quarterly* 12 at 12–13.

22 Ibid.

23 Board of Taxation 'Review of the Tax Arrangements Applying to managed investment trusts, a report to the Assistant Treasurer', August 2009, paragraph 2.1 page 9.

24 See generally *Tax Laws Amendment (New Tax System for Managed Investment Trusts) Act 2016* (Cth).

the regime predates the report)[25] this regime now provides the taxation framework expected to apply to any new vehicles introduced into the Australian environment.[26]

The new breed of collective investment vehicles – moving away from trusts

The *Johnson Report's* recommendation was articulated clearly in relation to the new collective investment vehicles:

> Clients and fund managers require an investment vehicle that provides a flow-through of any tax liabilities from the vehicle to the end investor, and has other investor protection and commercial needs. Australia's tax law in effect limits the range of commercial vehicles that can be used to manage funds to that of a unit trust, because only unit trusts provide tax flow-through and only unit trusts typically meet investor protection and commercial needs.[27]

The report went further, to explain why the trust structure could be holding Australian back:

> Many potential non-resident investors in Australian funds, particularly in the Asia-Pacific region, do not come from common law jurisdictions. Neither they nor investment advisers in the region are typically familiar or comfortable with trust structures. They are more familiar with managed funds structured as a corporate vehicle or a limited partnership. The lack of widespread use or recognition of unit trusts in the region contributes to Australian based funds management companies typically using collective investment vehicles that are established and administered offshore, such as in Luxembourg, Dublin or the Cayman Islands, and in some cases also basing their fund managers offshore. This is expensive, time consuming and not in Australia's interests. It results in employment in areas such as fund administration, accounting, legal, custody and other services being lost to offshore centres, with consequent loss of tax revenue in Australia.[28]

On 9 May 2016, the Coalition government committed to introduce two new collective investment vehicles (CIV) as part of its 'Ten Year Enterprise Tax Plan'. Announced as part of the 2016/17 Budget, the commitment was to introduce a corporate CIV for income years starting on or after 1 July 2017 and a limited

---

25 The Board of Taxation was asked to review the tax arrangements applying to managed-investment trusts in February 2008: <http://taxboard.gov.au/consultation/tax-arrangements-applying-to-managed-investment-trusts/>.

26 See for example Nat Raju *The tax 'wish list' for the CIV regime* (20 July 2017): <https://home.kpmg.com/au/en/home/insights/2017/07/the-tax-wish-list-20-july-2017.html>.

27 Johnson Report, above n4 at 62.

28 Ibid.

partnership CIV for income years starting on or after 1 July 2018.[29] This was a direct response to the *Johnson Report's* recommendation to develop a broader range of tax flow-through collective investment vehicles.[30]

Minister for Revenue and Financial Services, the Honourable Kelly O'Dwyer, in her July 2017 address to the industry, said of the corporate collective investment vehicle 'acknowledging its importance and potential, the Government will shortly consult on core elements of draft legislation to give effect to the new CCIV regulatory framework, with similar steps on a new tax framework to follow.'[31] At the time of writing public consultation on a preliminary draft bill which outlined the design of a corporate CIV had concluded and draft legislation for taxation rules and consequential legislative amendments had been released for initial consultation; with further drafts of both anticipated.

The government specifically consulted on the withholding taxation arrangements for collective investment vehicles in November 2016, in response to industry concerns that 'the current withholding tax regime will inhibit the sector's international competitiveness and reduce the effectiveness of the proposed vehicles'.[32] However the results of this consultation have not yet been released. In her July 2017 address, Minister O'Dwyer noted, 'We understand how important this issue is and are working to resolve it in the near future.'[33]

The funds management industry is eagerly awaiting these new vehicles and they will be a critical component in Australia's participation in the Asia Region Funds Passport.

Funds passporting – unlocking the region

A centrepiece of the *Johnson Report* was the recommendation to develop a multilateral Passport regime within the Asian region.[34] The idea was to develop an arrangement similar to the European Union's highly successful Undertaking for Collective Investment in Transferrable Securities which was established by a European Union

---

29 Ten Year Enterprise Tax Plan – implementing a new suite of collective investment vehicles Budget Paper 2: <http://www.budget.gov.au/2016-17/content/bp2/html/bp2_revenue-10.htm>.

30 Johnson Report, above n4, Recommendation 3.3.

31 The Hon Kelly O'Dwyer Speech 'Address to the Financial Services Council Leaders' Summit, International Convention Centre, Sydney' (26 July 2017): <http://kmo.ministers.treasury.gov.au/speech/015-2017/>.

32 The Hon. Kelly O'Dwyer, Consultation on collective investment vehicle non-resident withholding taxes Press Release (3 November 2016): <http://kmo.ministers.treasury.gov.au/media-release/098-2016/>.

33 Kelly O'Dwyer, above n31.

34 Johnson Report, Recommendation 4.3 above n4 at 87.

directive in 1985.[35] This Undertaking offers a structure whereby funds licensed in one country can be marketed to investors in any other country in Europe. Without this kind of arrangement fund operators would usually be required to set up a physical presence in the other jurisdiction in order to meet the relevant local licensing requirements.

For regional investors, passporting creates relatively instant access to a wide range of investment products, resulting in more options to diversify investment exposure and greater competition to drive down investment management fees. Australian investors would likewise have access to more offshore investment options, which is essential for a growing pool of investment funds that has already outstripped its domestic stock market.[36]

The original recommendation of the *Johnson Report* was to progress bilateral mutual-recognition agreements between Australia and its neighbours, and then work toward a passporting arrangement once these were in place. However the passporting concept has progressed ahead of bilateral mutual recognition. This is likely to be due to the expected regional benefits of a passporting regime. Research conducted by the APEC policy unit notes that increasing consumer access to a broader range of investment funds could result in significant savings for investors in the Asian region.[37]

The Asia Region Funds Passport (ARFP) has been developed by APEC through its group of Finance Ministers and is expected to be operational by 1 January 2018.[38] Signatories to the Memorandum of Cooperation for the Passport include Australia, New Zealand, South Korea, Japan and Thailand.

Passporting versus mutual recognition

Under a passporting arrangement participating regulators undertake due diligence on each other's regulatory frameworks to ensure that they are satisfied with the

---

35 European Commission, *UCITS – Undertakings for the collective investment in transferable securities* (2014): <http://ec.europa.eu/internal_market/investment/ucits-directive/index_en.htm>.

36 Market capitalisation of the Australian stock exchange is currently $1.5 trillion (ASX Corporate Overview http://www.asx.com.au/about/corporate-overview.htm) in comparison to the funds under management of $2.8 trillion reported by ABS (above n4).

37 Research conducted by APEC Policy Support Unit on the benefits to the Asian region shows the Asia Region funds Passport could improving efficiency, saving investors USD 20 billion per annum in fund management costs. China was included in the research despite it not currently being a signatory to the Passport. *Asia Region Funds Passport-A Study of Potential Economic Benefits and Costs* (July 2014): <http://publications.apec.org/publication-detail.php?pub_id=1535>.

38 For details see the dedicated APEC website for the Asia Region Funds Passport and the Memorandum of Cooperation <http://fundspassport.apec.org>.

level of regulation. A common set of rules are agreed to prevent the opportunity for regulatory arbitrage due to differences in levels of qualification or experience between the jurisdictions' 'home' rules. The rules cover both the threshold licence requirements and the allowable product features for a passportable fund. The home regulator is responsible for licensing the provider and products under both its home rules and the agreed passporting rules. Once the passporting approval is received the provider is free to operate in the other participating jurisdiction with only a streamlined or minimal approval process required by the host regulator.

Importantly the rules for passporting only extend to the production of fund investments (manufacture) and they do not extend to distribution. Depending on the host country requirements, it may still be necessary for the operator to either become licensed to sell fund products in the host jurisdiction or to have a commercial relationship with another entity that does. Further it is expected that a fund offered into a host jurisdiction will meet relevant local consumer protection rules regarding product disclosure.

In addition to the ARFP, an ASEAN Passport was initiated by Singapore, Malaysia and Thailand and has been operational since the Handbook for Collective Investment Schemes (CIS) Operators of ASEAN CISs was published on 25 August 2014.[39] Review of the respective regulators' websites shows the ASEAN Passport has not yet received much take-up.

Mutual recognition

Mutual recognition refers to bilateral agreement between two countries. Similar to passporting, mutual recognition of investment funds removes the need for an investment fund operator to obtain a licence from a new market in which it intends to operate and is facilitated by regulators from both jurisdictions coming to an agreement on the acceptability of each other's regulatory structures and systems. Regulators then agree to allow operators access to their market without additional licensing requirements; however mutual recognition usually requires a greater level of signoff from the host regulator than a passporting arrangement. Mutual recognition can also be subject to greater 'behind the border' barriers imposed in host jurisdictions as, unlike a passporting arrangement, there is no commonly agreed framework.

Australian examples of mutual recognition

Australia and New Zealand established mutual recognition of fund product offer documentation in 2011.[40] This arrangement has been largely facilitated by the

39 ASEAN, 'CIS Handbook' (25 August 2014): <http://www.theacmf.org/ACMF/upload/asean_cis_handbook.pdf>.

40 See ASIC Regulatory Guide 190: Offering securities in New Zealand and Australia

regulatory similarities between Australia and New Zealand. Whilst the regime has been successful, it is difficult to extrapolate from this example to mutual recognition agreements between Australia and China due to the regulatory similarities that exist between New Zealand and Australia.

Australia and Hong Kong established a mutual recognition agreement to overcome regulatory incompatibility issues in 2008.[41] Despite this agreement covering retail fund offerings little cross-border activity appears to occur between Hong Kong and Australia through the arrangement. It is unclear why this regime has not been successful. Hong Kong's positioning predominantly as a fund distribution centre into China may mean it is not an attractive retail market in itself for Australian fund manufacturers.

ASIC has established a 'regulatory equivalence' program that allows foreign managers to apply for recognition of the licence they hold in their home jurisdiction.[42] This approach is different from mutual recognition as it does not require involvement of the home regulator. If ASIC deems the manager's home regulation to have a requisite level of regulatory equivalence then it will recognise the home licence and allow the licensee to provide services to Australian wholesale investors. Notably the program does not extend to allow services to be provided to retail investors. This program is currently under review.

China and Hong Kong mutual recognition

A mutual recognition scheme operates for investment funds between China and Hong Kong. Under this regime Hong Kong-domiciled funds authorised by the Hong Kong Securities and Futures Commission benefit from a streamlined approval program from the China Securities Regulatory Commission.[43] Whilst there is a still a level of sign-off or authorisation required by the host jurisdiction, mutual recognition removes the need to operate a duplicate business in China.

Where to from here? Will trusts die out?

It is unlikely that trusts will die out in Australia in the foreseeable future. Despite greater offshore market access for Australian investment managers and a possible increase in the number of foreign funds available in Australia, Australian investors are used to trusts. Trusts have a firm grip on the Australian market, they underpin the trillions of dollars in superannuation savings and for large institutional investors

---

under mutual recognition, reissued 25 July 2017.

41 ASIC Class Order [CO 08/506] Hong Kong Investment Schemes.

42 See ASIC Regulatory Guide 176: Licensing: Discretionary powers – wholesale foreign financial services providers, issued 29 June 2012.

43 See SEC website for further details <http://www.sfc.hk/web/EN/faqs/mainland-hong-kong-mutual-recognition-of-funds.html>.

there is no reason to move from trusts structures.

For those managers looking to move offshore and attract foreign investors there may, however, be a move away from trusts. It is clear that they are not well understood and to have the greatest chance of success under the ARFP and any future bilateral mutual arrangements that Australia enters into, it may be necessary to offer products through one of the new collective investment vehicles. This may result in a proliferation of new vehicles and a future environment where trusts, corporate collective investment vehicles and limited partnership collective investment vehicles coexist.

The greatest risk that the Australian market faces is the failure of the government to either introduce the new vehicles in a timely manner or to provide globally competitive features in their design. It will be up to the industry to make its voice heard and ensure the benefits that could flow to consumers, both within Australia and the region, are realised.

Chapter 3

Start-ups Legal and Business Issues: The Entrepreneurial Perspective

William Page

Technology start-ups are, by their very nature, dynamic and ever-changing entities that can grow from a small team of one or more founders to possibly becoming the next 'tech giant' employing thousands of people. During the early months and years of a start-up's existence, it often operates as a true entrepreneurial venture with little or no formal corporate structure in place. Yet this dynamic approach can be difficult for the founders to maintain as the business grows larger and more complex. In time, the right systems, structures and processes need to be put in place by the founders to enable the start-up to grow and become a successful (and usually profitable) business. These systems, structures and processes need to be compatible with the culture of the start-up in order to successfully blend creativity and innovation with the stability needed for a start-up to reach its full potential and to prosper.

This chapter will focus on some of the structural and legal issues common to start-ups setting up in Australia and in the United Kingdom: jurisdictions chosen because they are where my professional and entrepreneurial experience is greatest. However, many of the issues raised in this chapter concerning establishing and expanding a start-up, are common to start-ups generally. The chapter will examine the early development of a start-up and provide guidance on some of the essential legal considerations that founders need to be aware of. It will then examine the issues and risks that founders face as they increase their businesses. And finally, it will provide recommendations for ways in which founders can successfully build their businesses whilst also maintaining control.

Life Cycle of the Typical Start-up

To succeed over time, a start-up will need to progress through various stages of the business life cycle. Along this journey, the founders will encounter different challenges that require legal and financial solutions as highlighted in Figure 1 below. These legal and financial challenges can take place early or late in the business cycle, depending on several variables, such as the nature of the start-up and the leadership of the founders.

Figure 1. Stages of start-up life cycle

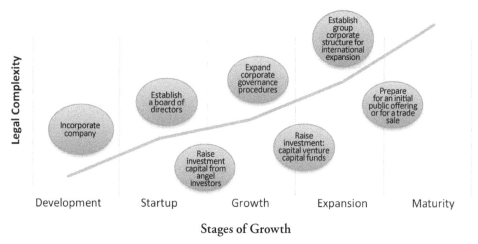

Stages of Growth

During the earliest development stages of the start-up, there may be little need to have formal legal systems or processes in place. As the business expands, it is normal practice in many countries to incorporate a company to allow the business to take advantage of what corporatisation can offer (such as limited liability, transparency, the ability to raise capital etc.)[1]. Directors who are concerned about the financial position of their company should keep a careful track of its finances and actions and also take specialist advice from accountants and lawyers to ensure that the company is not trading whilst insolvent.

In time, governance systems and processes need to be put in place to manage the growing operations of the company and of its team. As the company expands internationally, a new, more sophisticated (and possibly tiered) corporate structure may need to be established to manage the interactions of the different component parts of the ever-growing business.

In less than a year, a start-up can grow dramatically from being just an idea to having a turnover of millions of dollars. The proven potential for such rapid growth

---

1 In doing so the founders are able to benefit from the legal precedent set by the English courts in *Salomon's Case* [1897] AC 22 (and refined by subsequent cases including *Macaura* v *Northern Assurance Co* [1925] AC 619, *Lee* v *Lee's Air Farming Limited* [1960] UKPC 33 and the Farrar case: *Farrar* v *Farrars Ltd* (1888) 40 ChD 395) that a company is a separate legal entity and thus a juristic 'person' in the eyes of the law with a separate legal personality from that of the owners, members, or shareholders. In doing so the founders of the company are protected by 'the corporate veil', which shields the founders and their personal assets from individual liability for corporate acts in relation to the company. This protection is only pierced with the directors facing personal liability in certain exceptional circumstances, such as trading whilst the company is insolvent, which is an offence under s588G *Corporations Act 2001* in Australia and s214 *Insolvency Act 1986* in the UK.

and success should give new founders hope that they too can build something substantial from the ground up in a relatively short period of time. However, founders will need to constantly adapt and change the structure of the start-up as the business grows, new opportunities present themselves and perhaps even the very nature of the business changes. By keeping up and engaging with changes in their industry and business processes, aspiring founders will be able to harness new opportunities as and when they arise.

Crucially, as the start-up expands, the founders need to have one eye on the future: the challenges and opportunities that the business will face. Whether the plan is for the business to be kept for the long term, privately sold or listed on a stock exchange, steps and procedures need to be put in place to enable the business to succeed and cope with the changes that will result. Having the right systems and processes in place early on will enable changes to be undertaken more easily, possibly more cost-effectively, and should provide comfort and reassurance to possible future investors and partners.

Incorporating a company

Founders establishing a new start-up business are responsible for deciding upon and initiating the organisation's structure[2]. In doing so they decide upon the purpose of the organisation and whether it will be to generate economic returns or if there are other goals, for example social or environmental goals. These early decisions are often crucial in shaping the culture, identity, future structure and direction of the business.

So what influences the choice of structure used by the founders? Well, the founders need to consider:

    (i)   their personal liability exposure from the business products or services;
    (ii) whether or not they plan to have partners or investors in the business in the future;
    (iii) the administrative costs of setting up and maintaining a given business structure, and
    (iv) the tax effectiveness of the business structure.

Although there are a number of options available to the founders, ranging from being a sole trader (in the case of a single founder) to being a partnership (where there are multiple founders), the most common practice in both the UK and in Australia is to establish a private company limited by shares (Limited Co). In the UK this is in the form of a 'Limited Company' (indicated by the suffix 'Ltd') whilst in Australia it is known as a 'Proprietary Limited Company' (indicated by the suffix 'Pty Limited').

---

2 A Stinchecombe, 'Social structure and organization' in J.G. March (ed.), *Handbook of Organizations* (New York: Rand McNally, 1965) at 142–93.

One of the main benefits of a Limited Co. is that the start-up is recognised as being a legal entity separate from the founders. As the name suggests, under a Limited Co. the founders' liability is limited to their capital investment in the business and, more generally, to the share capital paid up by the shareholders. This corporate structure protects the founders' personal assets and only the company assets are at risk in the event of any legal action against or default by the Limited Co. If they wish to do so, it also has the flexibility to enable the founders to raise capital from external investors by bringing them in as new shareholders. However, incorporating a Limited Co. does require the satisfaction of certain formalities, there are costs involved and a Limited Co. can be relatively expensive to maintain compared to other business structures.

The Need to Establish a Board of Directors

Once the company has been incorporated, the founders need to establish a board of directors to manage the company. The board can consist of one or more people and will ultimately be responsible for making the critical decisions for the company, such as how to raise investment capital, how best to develop the business and whether to enter into important strategic transactions. It is crucial that the board consists of people who are knowledgeable about the business and the industry in which the business operates or who otherwise bring business acumen and additional skills that may benefit the company and the founders.

Legal Responsibilities of Directors

Company directors owe fiduciary duties to the shareholders. The directors are entrusted with managing the business which is owned by different people. Historically, these duties were only outlined under common law but in recent years there has been a move by the legislature in many countries to codify these rules into legislation in an effort to encourage better corporate governance practices. Founders need to be aware of these duties and ensure that they act in accordance with them. These duties are now codified in legislation, namely the *Corporations Act 2001* in Australia and the *Companies Act 2006* in the UK.[3]

---

3 In the UK there are seven key duties for directors in relation to their company that are found in the *Companies Act 2006*. These duties reflect the common law and equitable principles, namely: i) to act within their powers (s171); ii) to promote the success of the company (s172); iii) to exercise independent judgment (s173); iv) to exercise reasonable care, skill and diligence (s174); v) to avoid conflicts of interest (s175); vi) not to accept benefits from third parties (s176); and vii) to declare interest in proposed transaction or arrangement (s177). Australia also has similar fiduciary responsibilities that derive from many English and common law cases and that are now found in the *Corporations Act 2001*. These duties include: i) care and diligence (s180); ii) to act in good faith (s181); iii) not to improperly use their position to gain an advantage for themselves or someone else or to the detriment to the

Company directors need to be aware that their fiduciary responsibilities are to all shareholders in the company, not just to their own interests or to specific groups of shareholders. Failure to act in the best interests of all shareholders can leave the directors liable to punishment including being banned from acting as a director, fines and, in some cases, custodial sentences.

These duties are owed to the company and only the company will be able to enforce them, although in certain circumstances shareholders may be able to bring a derivative action on the company›s behalf. As the company expands, the founders should arrange for the company to purchase insurance to provide protection for directors against any personal liability in connection with any negligence, default, breach of duty or breach of trust by them in relation to that company. Figure 2 outlines the key issues that founders need to consider initially, in forming their legal entity and in subsequently planning for the future of their business.

Figure 2. Issues to consider during formation of a start-up

Raising Capital

During the early life of many start-ups it is common for founders to grow their company by using only the company's cash flow and being cautious with their expenses. This process is known as 'bootstrapping'. It enables the founders to maintain control of their company without having to worry about external investors whose interests and goals may be very different from those of the founders. However, in doing so the founders are likely to have limited capital to put towards growing the business.

There are several possible sources of capital ranging from traditional finance from 'angel investors' and the banks, through to newer forms of raising capital such as crowd funding from the general public. In practice, it is unlikely that founders will be able to access bank finance during the early years of their start-up as they will have a limited track record and insufficient collateral in the business. Depending on the jurisdiction of the raise there are also legal limitations on raising capital from

---

company (s182); and iv) not to improperly use the information they gain in the course of their director duties to gain an advantage for themselves or someone else or to the detriment to the company (s183).

the general public through crowd funding; the legal and regulatory requirements of doing a raise are still being finalised in many countries. For these reasons, founders tend to seek capital from private angel investors.

Founders will typically seek outside investors to invest in the business so that it can grow at a faster rate than would otherwise be achievable and also to try to attract new talent who can provide skills that the founders don't have. If the founders do decide to seek to raise external capital from investors, such as angel investors and venture capital funds, and are successful in doing so, then there are documents that are usually required for the fundraising. The main documentation includes:

(a). *A subscription and shareholders' agreement.* This will contain:
- the terms on which the investor makes its investment, the equity it gets for the investment and how the investment will be made (i.e. in a single investment or through series of tranches upon certain key performance indicators being met);
- warranties provided by the target company and its founders as to the position of the company and, to a limited extent, the founders' other business interests;
- restrictive covenants provided by the founders;
- a series of obligations as to the management and governance of the company and matters which specifically require investor consent.

(b) *Articles of association* that deal with:
- the rights attaching to shares;
- new share issues and transfers;
- the operation of the board; and
- general constitutional matters.

(c) *Service agreements.* The founders and the wider management team need to have service or employment agreements in place with the company.

Within the subscription and shareholders' agreement, it is common for certain share transfer restrictions to be included in order to ensure that all shareholders stand and exit together through any sale in order to maximise overall shareholder value. Typical terms included in the subscription and shareholders' agreement include:

- *Pre-emption rights on transfer.* The articles of association will almost certainly contain pre-emption rights that prevent shareholders from transferring their shares to third parties in most circumstances, unless they have first offered those shares to existing shareholders on the same terms.
- *Tag-along rights.* This prohibits share transfers to third parties that would result in a third party holding a controlling interest in the company, unless that third party has offered to acquire all shareholders' shares on the same terms.
- *Drag-along rights.* This prevents a shareholder from transferring a proportion of his shareholding to a third party, unless all shareholders

have been given the right to transfer a similar proportion of their shares to that buyer on the same terms.

There are three other key areas within the subscription and shareholders' agreement that founders need to pay careful attention to and where possible negotiate:

- *Special shareholder approvals.* Shareholder agreements usually provide certain groups of shareholders with specific approvals over certain fundamental corporate changes. Typical examples include making changes to the articles of association of the company or approving the sale of the company. Founders need to ensure that the circumstances where shareholder approval is required are not too onerous, otherwise their ability to effectively manage the business may be frustrated.
- *Anti-dilution protection.* These provisions are included to protect investors against the diluting effects of a down-round reflecting a decrease in the valuation of the company. Typically the protected shareholders acquire additional shares issued at a nominal value, thereby reducing the diluting effect on them. All existing shareholders will still be affected if new shareholders subscribe for shares, but the anti-dilution provisions will reduce the dilution in shareholding value. Such provisions usually provide either a full-ratchet protection or weighted-average ratchet protection, depending on the extent to which they reduce the average share price paid by the shareholders who benefit from the protection. A full ratchet anti-dilution clause essentially states that if the company ever issues shares at a lower cost than the venture capitalist invested at, the company will automatically issue more shares to the venture capitalist to bring their investment to the share price of the down-round. Founders should always avoid accepting a full ratchet. It can result in founders ending up with very little of their business if subsequent down-rounds occur at a later date. It also shifts the risk from the venture capitalist to the other shareholders as there is little risk for the venture capitalist in accepting a high valuation at the funding round, and then an incentive to push for a low valuation in future funding rounds, investing heavily and taking a large chunk of the company in the process.
- *Liquidation preferences.* This is a risk reduction tool used in the event that the business fails but still has value in it, or used to give particular shareholders a superior return over others if there is a profitable sale of the business. The clause outlines how the remaining value of the company is to be shared between the equity owners when a liquidation occurs. This could be a negative event such as bankruptcy or it could also be any other time where shareholders receive money for giving up equity, for example on a trade sale occurring.

Leaving the company

It is common for the articles of association to provide that if a founder leaves the company, then the founder is automatically required to offer to sell his or her shares to the remaining shareholders. It is not uncommon for leavers to be paid different prices for their shares, depending on the reasons for their leaving the company. Such reasons are typically broken down into:

- Bad leavers commonly get a restricted price for their shares. Bad leavers are usually employee shareholders who leave before an agreed period of time or have done something wrong but within their control (for example, a breach of their employment contract, poor performance or gross misconduct).
- Good leavers usually get fair market value for their shares. Good leavers are usually employee shareholders who leave after an agreed period of time and/or have otherwise done nothing wrong.

The investment agreement and the founders' employment or service agreement also commonly contain restrictive covenants that stipulate that the founders will commit their full time and attention to the business to the exclusion of any other business opportunity. It is common for there to also be provisions stipulating that should the founders leave the business, they will not work for or be involved with any competing business for an agreed period and will not try to take away any of the investee company›s employees, customers, suppliers or other key business contacts.

The Founders Need to Maintain Control

If the founders are successful in raising external capital they will typically have to cede some ownership of the company and, to a certain extent, some decision-making power. This can lead to a trade-off occurring between the founders trying to maintain control of the company they started and the desire to build a company with a higher value.

The greatest pressure on founders at an early stage of a start-up business will come from angel investors and venture capital funds. Venture capital funds, and to a lesser extent angel investors, will often push for one or more nominated directors to be appointed by them to join the company's board. They will do this in order that their interests be represented on the board and so that they are more involved and engaged in the company's business and activities. This may also provide them with greater oversight of the activities of the founders. Whilst it may bring greater experience to the board in the form of a seasoned director, it will also mean that the founders lose some control over the management of the company. If they lose control of the board, this leaves the founders vulnerable to being fired if the investors are no longer happy with the founders' leadership or if the founder makes too many mistakes.

Every time investors invest in the company, the founders will have to negotiate terms, which, for substantial investors, usually includes agreement on the composition of the board. These terms will usually be stated in a shareholders' agreement or in a voting agreement. These agreements often lock in the number of directors and designate who controls the various board seats. Quite often, new investors will demand changes, such as their own board seat or a reduction in board seats that the founders' control. Over time this reduces the power and control that the founders have over the board.

Tips for Maintaining Control

So how can the founders push back and defend their interests? Firstly, the founders should try to ensure that they always control a majority of the seats on the board. If this is not possible, then the founders should designate that at least one seat is to be held by an 'independent' person. This person is typically not an investor or a founder or an employee of the company, but should have industry knowledge and valuable contacts. So, for example, by appointing an independent director after the second or third round of investments, the composition of the board could be the two founders, two investor representatives and the independent director. This would ensure that the independent director would resolve any tiebreak.

Secondly, the founders can try to put transparent systems and processes in place so that the investors can see that the founders appreciate good corporate governance and feel that the founders can be trusted to run a tight ship. Examples include having all legal documentation (i.e. employment agreements, investment documentation, board minutes, expenses) properly documented, properly signed and stored in an organised and efficient manner, available for inspection should the need arise, and to ensure that all financial reporting and the accounts are up-to-date and regularly verified.

Thirdly, founders should ensure that they spend sufficient time vetting potential independent board members. The independent directors should not be connected to the investors and preferably be sufficiently independent that they are unlikely to be unduly swayed or biased by the investors. The founders should carry out extensive interviews and due diligence on the independent directors to understand their background, voting record on other boards (where applicable), industry experience and rationale for wanting to join the board.

Fourthly, prior to worrying about board composition, the founders need to choose investors in the company whom they believe they will enjoy working with. If investors are difficult or troublesome when negotiating the initial investment, it is likely that they will also be difficult to work with once invested. It is crucial that, as the business scales up, the founders have a good working relationship with the investors and their appointed directors; this way they avoid any potential issues at the board level and secure their leadership of the company that they founded.

Fifthly, it is vital for founders to anticipate the investor's expectations and where possible get ahead of them. Investor directors on a board will often highlight what is missing and use that as a foundation from which to complain about the product or the leadership of the company. Consequently, founders need to understand the investor's concerns and what they are looking for and try to mitigate them well in advance of any board meetings. In doing so they strengthen their position in meetings and provide comfort to investors about the founders' management of the company.

Finally, founders should put in place, as early as possible, board rules and governance policies (i.e. minimum number of meetings, quorum), even if they don't have any investors at the time. By doing this early in the company life cycle, when possible investment is considered, the founders are able to dictate the terms thus giving them a better negotiating position: existing systems will already be in place.

Use of Different Share Classes

Founders can use different share classes as a way to maintain shareholder-voting control of the company, even when they only control a minority equity interest in the company. Depending on the jurisdiction of incorporation and whether the company is listed or not, it is possible for companies to have different classes of shares.[4]

Each class of shares comes with a different set of rights for shareholders. The most common practice is to issue two classes of shares, Class A (ordinary) shares and Class B (preference) shares. The rights attached to these classes can vary greatly but founders will typically get 10 votes or 100 votes for each Class A share they own, whilst Class B shares might give shareholders 1 vote for each Class B share they own. This has led to the Class A shares often being called 'super-voting shares' as they enable the founders to continue to maintain shareholder control. This is a more common practice in the US where dual-class shareholdings are allowed in public companies and where founders, executives and any other key stakeholders have enough super-voting shares to help them retain control over the company. In most cases, these super-voting shares are not publicly traded and company founders and their families are most commonly the controlling groups in dual-class companies.

---

4 The NYSE, Nasdaq Stock Market, Toronto Stock Exchange and Nasdaq OMX Stockholm permit listed companies to use dual-class structures. Whilst dual-class listings are technically possible for a premium share listing in the UK, the regulatory requirements that controlling shareholders have to follow and the minority protection rights put in place make such listings extremely rare and difficult to undertake. Other exchanges including the Australia Securities Exchange, the Singapore Stock Exchange and the Stock Exchange of Hong Kong (HKEx) do not typically permit companies with dual-class structures to be listed, although there have been some discussions about introducing the option. Alibaba, which is the Chinese e-commerce with a market capitalisation of over US$350 million, considered listing on the HKEx but decided to list in the US on the NYSE as it wanted to allow its founders and top management to nominate most board members despite holding a minority stake, which conflicted with the one-share-one-vote principle strictly enforced by the HKEx.

This structure also has other less obvious benefits. Concentrating voting rights among a particular class of shareholders makes a takeover attempt more difficult as the company can choose to sell to the public only its regular shares with lesser voting rights. Founders also often have a longer-term vision than investors who may be focused on the most recent quarterly figures, so this gives the company a longer-term approach to growth rather than focussing on short-term benefits. However, super-voting shares only work if founders have enough leverage to negotiate favourable terms at each round of financing. Historically, family-controlled companies (such as NewsCorp) used such structures; however, new technology companies with strong founder leadership such as Groupon, LinkedIn, Facebook and Atlassian are increasingly using these structures to enable founders to maintain control. Many international start-ups, such as Australian-based Atlassian, have listed on the New York Stock Exchange (NYSE) and the Nasdaq specifically to benefit from the exchanges allowing dual-class structures.

Facebook provides a great example of founders successfully using this structure to maintain control once their company has been listed. Facebook's A-class shares give co-founder Mark Zuckerberg super-voting power that allows him to maintain control over the company, even as he sold shares to venture capitalists and in Facebook's public offering. Zuckerberg also benefitted from negotiating with investors to give him their votes as a proxy, so that he was able to maintain voting control over a substantial number of shares that were not owned by him.

So how was Zuckerberg able to negotiate such arrangements? Well, by creating a great company with considerable traction, Zuckerberg was able to negotiate with investors from a position of strength and had the ability to walk away from any deal that he didn't like. In doing so, he was able to obtain considerable concessions from investors. By also giving examples of the missteps that Facebook could have made, he was able to show the benefits of the structure where the founders had control. For example, in 2006, Yahoo offered to buy Facebook for around US$1 billion, an offer that Zuckerberg probably would have been pressured by his investors to accept. However, by holding steadfast and refusing the offer Zuckerberg was able to focus on growing the company and the US$100 billion + valuation of the company indicates that such strong founder leadership has paid off handsomely for Facebook's investors.

Interestingly there has recently been a backlash against dual-class listings as questions are raised over their corporate governance and they are seen as being unfair for ordinary investors. On 1 August 2017, Standard & Poor's 500 index announced that it was no longer allowing companies with dual-class share structures to join its index, which is one of the largest and most respected US indices.[5] This decision was

---

5 John Devine, *Karma for SNAP Stock: S&P 500 Bans Dual-Class Shares* (1 August 2017): <https://money.usnews.com/investing/stock-market-news/articles/2017-08-01/snap-stock-s-p-500-bans-dual-class-shares>.

partly taken as a result of the listing of the new tech company Snap on the NYSE. It raised US$3.4 billion with not a single share issued in the IPO having voting rights. Snap subsequently saw a decline in its share price with many questioning its corporate governance practices and considering it to be disrespectful to public shareholders.[6] Whether other exchanges and indices will follow Standard & Poor's lead on this remains to be seen.

Voting Provisions

Aside from creating different types of shares, founders can also negotiate on other rights that investors would get. Typically, investors would expect to be given some protective voting provisions, such as voting blocks on acquisitions or on future equity financings. By eliminating these voting-control provisions, founders have the freedom to dictate when and whether the company sells or raises capital. Venture capital funds will always receive some voting protections in their investment documents, but these provisions are increasingly limited to preserving negotiated-for rights of the investors, such as the preferred capital return and liquidation rights.

Founder Vesting Provisions

It is also common for investors to push for founders to have their existing shares vest or crystallise over a period of time after they invest. They do this to ensure that the founders remain committed to the company and do not leave it after the investors have invested. It is crucial for founders to negotiate that these vesting provisions occur as soon as is possible. Standard vesting clauses typically last three or four years and have a one-year 'cliff'. This means that if a founder had 50 per cent equity and leaves after two years then they will only retain 25 per cent in the company. The longer the founder stays, the larger the percentage of their equity that will be vested until they become fully vested, for example in the 48th month (four years) if the vesting period is four years. Each month that the founder actively works full time in the company, a 1/48th of the founder's total equity package will vest. However, because they have a one-year 'cliff', if one of the founders leaves the company before the 12th month, then he or she walks away with nothing; whereas staying until day 366 means that the founder gets one quarter of their stocks vested instantly. The unvested shares held by the founder become subject to a contractual right of repurchase, often at a nominal value, if the founder is no longer providing services to the company.

Let's take the example of a company that has already gained some traction and raised a seed round from angel investors during its 12th month. If there were two

6 Anita Balakrishnan, *Snap is falling again as Wall Street worries about the company's corporate structure* (1 August 2017): < https://www.cnbc.com/2017/08/01/snapchat-excluded-from-sp-500-what-does-it-mean.html>.

founders, each with 40 per cent equity and angel investors holding the other 20 per cent then a founder walking away would have only a 10 per cent equity shareholding vested as only one year had passed. So what happens to the remaining 30 per cent? Well, the shares disappear after the company has repurchased them from the exiting founder. This would reduce the number of shares in circulation and have the knock-on effect of increasing the percentage shareholding that the remaining shareholders would have in the company.

The Risk of Dilution

There are very few examples of successful founders owning 100 per cent of their companies at the time of a trade sale or IPO: typically because the founders will have diluted their shareholding by raising earlier financing rounds. Depending on the time and nature of these rounds, investors commonly obtain equity ranging from a few per cent to possibly 50 per cent + equity in a company: each time further diluting the equity and control of the founders. Founders' share will also be diluted if they establish an employee share-option scheme, which is typically required by investors and is also viewed as a way to encourage the employees to assist in growing the company.

Conclusion

We are very much living in a golden age of entrepreneurship as the costs of starting a business have dramatically come down, investment capital has become much more readily available and advances in today's technology and trends all enable more people to start a business than ever before. One of the most important features about companies and company law in general, is that founders have flexibility in how they structure their company and their operations. Although there are some legal limits on structures, company law drafters have developed legal and regulatory frameworks that meet the needs of founders and other stakeholders, such as investors.

Nevertheless, despite the benefits of technology and the comfort and support provided by company law, the road to being a successful founder of a start-up remains paved with difficulty and is still incredibly risky with 95 per cent of all start-ups failing in their first year.[7] This chapter has highlighted some of the key things that founders need to look out for as they start and grow a business. Founders should ensure that, from very early in the development of the business, they structure the company and the board in a way that makes sense for achieving their long-term goals and put in place good corporate governance as the business grows.

---

7 'The grim reality of start-ups: 95 per cent fail', *Sydney Morning Herald* (20 March 2015): <http://www.smh.com.au/business/the-grim-reality-of-start-ups-95-per-cent-fail-20150320-1m3wtb.html>.

When dealing with investors, founders need to read the relevant documentation carefully, negotiate heavily and avoid signing over-aggressive clauses that could weaken their leadership and shareholding in the future. By doing so, they will avoid potentially unfair and abusive provisions in their agreements that could become any entrepreneur's worst nightmare, namely to end up with very little or no control or ownership of the business that they conceived and fought so hard to build.

Chapter 4

The Concept of Attribution in Corporate Law: Making Corporations Liable for Criminal Conduct

Dr Juliette Overland

> *The attribution of criminal liability to corporations is an intractable subject; indeed, it is one of the blackest holes in criminal law.*[1]

Imposing criminal liability on corporations is a difficult concept, and a variety of legal mechanisms have been utilised in attempts to make corporations liable for criminal conduct. The common law has attempted to address the issue of corporate liability for crimes in two primary ways: through principles of vicarious liability and through direct liability. Specific statutory rules have also been developed to apply the elements of various criminal offences to corporations. In this paper, I consider the many legal rules that have developed to provide for corporate criminal liability, I examine the difficulties and challenges associated with the different mechanisms of attribution, and I discuss recent developments in this area.

Why is Corporate Attribution Necessary?

Corporations have been recognised as separate legal entities – independent of the natural persons who are their founders, promoters, directors, shareholders, employees, creditors and debtors – since the seminal case of Salomon v A Salomon and Co Ltd.[2] However, the law also recognises that while corporations are separate legal persons, they rely on individuals, usually their officers, agents, and employees, to represent them and act for them.

Unlike a natural person, a corporation clearly has no physical body or mind of its own, which caused Lord Chancellor Baron Thurlow to famously remark that 'corporations have neither bodies to be punished, nor souls to be condemned.'[3] However, this necessary reliance on natural persons by corporations has led to difficulties when seeking to make corporations criminally liable. Traditionally, under the common law, criminal offences were made up of two primary elements: an 'actus

---

1 Brent Fisse, 'The Attribution of Criminal Liability to Corporations: A Statutory Model' (1992) 13 *Sydney Law Review* 277 at 277.

2 [1897] AC 22.

3 John Poynder, *Literary Extracts* (1844) at 268.

reus' (a guilty act) and 'mens rea' (a guilty mind). These concepts were originally developed with individual offenders in mind[4], and have often proved difficult to apply to corporations.[5]

These difficulties have resulted in different approaches to corporate criminal liability. Some adopt the position of 'individualism', based on a view that criminal liability should only be imposed on natural persons, arguing that 'corporations don't commit offences, people do.'[6] This view is commonly justified on the basis that corporations cannot be imprisoned, that significant fines cause hardship to the shareholders of a corporation rather than to those within the corporation who carry out the relevant criminal acts or omissions, and that the imposition of punishments upon corporations does little to actually deter criminal activity.[7] An alternative position is that of 'collectivism', under which it is argued that corporations are more likely to take internal action to prevent relevant criminal conduct occurring, if corporations themselves may have liability for any resulting crime.[8] Proponents of collectivism believe that the existence of corporate criminal liability acts as a deterrent to those who might engage in criminal conduct within a corporation.[9] The third position is a middle-ground of 'liability of last resort', with corporate criminal liability considered to be appropriate only where no one individual can be identified as having criminal responsibility for the relevant acts or omissions.[10]

In Australia, it is generally accepted that it is appropriate to impose criminal liability on corporations as well as natural persons. By way of example, the *Criminal Code Act 1995* (Cth) (*Criminal Code*) provides in s. 12.1(b) that a 'body corporate may be found guilty of any offence, including one punishable by imprisonment.'

---

4 (NSW) Law Reform Commission, *Sentencing: Corporate Offenders,* Report No. 10 (2003) at [2.3].

5 Jonathan Clough and Carmel Mulhern, *The Prosecution of Corporations* (Oxford University Press, 2002) at 71.

6 Brent Fisse and John Braithwaite, 'The Allocation of Responsibility for Corporate Crime: Individualism, Collectivism and Accountability' (1988) 11 *Sydney Law Review* 469 at 473.

7 John C. Coffee, 'No Soul to Damn, No Body to Kick: An Unscandalized Inquiry into the Problem of Corporate Punishment' (1981) 79 *Michigan Law Review* 386 at 387–9; Simon Chesterman, 'The Corporate Veil, Crime and Punishment' (1994) 19 *Melbourne University Law Review* 1064 at 1072–3.

8 Clough and Mulhern, above n5; John C Coffee, 'Corporate Crime and Punishment: A Non-Chicago View of the Economics of Criminal Sanctions' (1980) *American Criminal Law Review* 419 at 421; Fisse and Braithwaite, above n6 at 489.

9 Fisse and Braithwaite, above n6 at 510.

10 See, for example, Lim Win Ts'ai, 'Corporations and the Devil's Dictionary: The Problem of Individual Responsibility for Corporate Crimes' (1990) 12 *Sydney Law Review* 311 at 313; Matthew Goode, 'Corporate Criminal Liability' in Neil Gunningham, Jennifer Norberry and Sandra McKillop (eds), *Environmental Crime (*Australian Institute of Criminology, 1995) at 6.

The Development of Corporate Attribution Principles

The first recorded cases of corporate criminal liability related to crimes of strict liability.[11] They concerned regulatory offences, such as criminal nuisance, which only required evidence that the relevant acts or omissions had occurred (the actus reus), without needing any proof of mens rea.[12] However, the common law later developed two primary models of corporate criminal liability: vicarious liability – where a corporation is liable for the criminal conduct of its officers or employees; and direct liability through the identification doctrine – where a corporation is regarded as having engaged in the criminal conduct itself due to the actions and intentions of its organs.[13]

Vicarious Liability

Vicarious liability is a form of indirect liability, which arises when one person has responsibility for the conduct of another, because of the nature of the relationship between them. Although vicarious liability is most commonly used in tort to impose liability for negligence, corporations can also be found vicariously liable for crimes committed by officers or employees acting within the scope of their employment or authority.[14] However, a corporation will generally only have vicarious criminal liability for crimes committed by its officers or employees where the crime is prohibited by statute, and where the statute indicates a clear legislative intent that such liability should be imposed on the corporation. In *Mousell Bros Ltd v London and North-Western Railway Co,*[15] Viscount Reading CJ stated that:

> Prima facie ... a master is not to be made criminally responsible for the acts of his servant to which the master is not a party. But it may be the intention of the legislature, in order to guard against the happening of the forbidden thing, to impose a liability upon a principal even though he does not know of, and is not a party to, the forbidden act done by his servant. Many statutes are passed with this object. In those cases the legislature absolutely forbids the act and makes the principal liable without a mens rea.[16]

Where vicarious criminal liability applies, the corporation is not regarded as having engaged in the offence itself, but it has liability for the crime due to the

---

11 For example, *R v Birmingham and Gloucester Railway Co* (1842) 114 ER 492; *R v The Great North of England Railway Co* (1846) 115 ER 1294.

12 Clough and Mulhern, above n5 at 72–3.

13 (NSW) Law Reform Commission, above n4 at [2.5].

14 Meaghan Wilkinson, 'Corporate Criminal Liability – The Move Towards Recognising Genuine Corporate Fault' (2003) 9 *Canterbury Law Review* 142.

15 [1917] 2 KB 836, applied by the High Court in *R v Australasian Films Ltd* (1921) 29 CLR 195.

16 *Mousell Bros Ltd v London and North-Western Railway Co* [1917] 2 KB 836 at 844.

relationship between the corporation and the person actually committing the offence. Accordingly, 'due diligence' defences, which provide that there is no liability where a corporation has taken reasonable precautions to prevent the relevant act or omission occurring, are often available under statutes which impose criminal vicarious liability.[17] Criminal vicarious liability is rarely imposed for serious offences, but is more commonly utilised for those that are regulatory in nature, such as fair-trading, consumer protection and environmental offences, where it would otherwise be impossible to enforce the law.[18]

Direct Liability

The common law model of the 'doctrine of identification'[19] operates to impose direct criminal liability on corporations, so that the actus reus and mens rea of certain officers or agents are taken to be those of the corporation.[20] The corporation is regarded as having committed the crime itself, rather than merely being held responsible for crimes committed by others.

The identification doctrine relies on the concept of the 'directing mind and will' of a corporation, which originated in the civil case of *Lennard's Carrying Co Ltd v Asiatic Petroleum Co Ltd,*[21] where Viscount Haldane LC famously stated:

> A corporation is an abstraction. It has no mind of its own any more than a body of its own; its active and directing will must consequently be sought in the person of somebody who ... may be called an agent, but who is really the directing mind and will of the corporation, the very ego and centre of the personality of the corporation.[22]

In *Tesco Supermarkets Ltd v Nattrass*[23] (*Tesco's case*) the principle of the 'directing mind and will' of a corporation was applied to criminal liability. In this case, Lord Reid approved the comments of Viscount Haldane LC[24] in *Lennard's Carrying Co Ltd v Asiatic Petroleum Co Ltd,*[25] noting that:

---

17 Fisse, above n1 at 279.

18 Clough and Mulhern, above n5 at 124.

19 Also known as 'organic theory' or the 'alter ego' doctrine: Ross Grantham, 'Attributing Responsibility to Corporate Entities: A Doctrinal Approach' (2001) 19 *Company and Securities Law Journal* 168 at 168; G R Sullivan, 'The Attribution of Culpability to Limited Companies' (1996) 55 *Cambridge Law Journal* 515 at 515.

20 Martin Wolff, 'On the Nature of Legal Persons' (1938) 54 *Law Quarterly Review* 494.

21 [1915] AC 705.

22 Ibid at 713–14.

23 (1972) AC 153.

24 Ibid at 170.

25 [1915] AC 705.

a corporation … must act through living persons, though not always one or the same person. Then the person who acts is not speaking or acting for the company. He is acting as the company and his mind which directs his acts is the mind of the company … He is an embodiment of the company … and his mind is the mind of the company. If it is a guilty mind then that guilt is the guilt of the company.[26]

The use of the identification doctrine to impose direct criminal liability on corporations has been accepted and applied in a number of Australian cases[27] and approved by the High Court in *Hamilton v Whitehead*.[28] However, there can be great difficulty in determining who may actually be regarded as the directing mind and will of a corporation. The directing mind and will may be, as stated by Lord Reid, the board of directors; the managing director; or a superior officer who 'carr[ies] out the functions of management and speak[s] and act[s] as the corporation.'[29] The concept does not apply to 'all servants of a company … who exercise some managerial discretion under the direction of superior officers'.[30] A person who is the directing mind and will of a corporation can only be a person or persons given 'full discretion to act independently of instruction' from the board.[31]

The decision in *Tesco's case* has since been criticised by the Privy Council in *Meridian Global Funds Management Asia Limited v Securities Commission*,[32] (*Meridian's case*) in which it was stated that the identification doctrine is only one form of attribution available to determine direct corporate criminal liability.[33] It was noted in *ABC Developmental Learning Centres Pty Ltd v Wallace*[34] that *Meridian's case* has 'been frequently followed or cited with approval in various contexts', but it was also recognised that each of these instances involved cases which were regulatory in nature.[35] Most importantly, the reasoning in *Meridian's case* has not been adopted by the High Court, whose approval of the 'identification doctrine'

---

26 *Tesco's case* n23 at 170.

27 See, for example, *Hanley v Automotive Food, Metals, Engineering, Printing and Kindred Industries Union* (2000) 100 FCR 530; *Collins v State Rail Authority (NSW)* (1986) 5 NSWLR 209; *Walplan Pty Ltd v Wallace* (1985) 8 FCR 27; *Trade Practices Commission v Tubemakers of Australia Ltd* (1983) 47 ALR 719; *G.J. Coles & Co Ltd v Goldsworthy* [1985] WAR 183; *Universal Telecasters (Qld) Ltd v Guthrie* (1978) 18 ALR 531.

28 (1988) 166 CLR 121.

29 *Tesco's case* at 171.

30 Ibid (Lord Reid).

31 Ibid (Lord Reid), at 193 (Lord Pearson).

32 [1995] AC 500.

33 *Meridian's case,* n32 at 507 (emphasis added).

34 [2006] VSC 171 (3 May 2006) at [6].

35 Ibid at [12].

in *Tesco's case* remains the definitive pronouncement on direct corporate criminal liability under the common law in Australia. Additionally, despite *Meridian's case,* the identification doctrine seems to have remained the judicially preferred basis for corporate attribution in relation to serious crimes involving mens rea.[36]

Statutory Principles of Corporate Criminal Liability

In addition to the common law rules, certain statutory regimes set out a variety of different statutory mechanisms for attributing criminal offences to corporations in the Commonwealth arena: including provisions concerning Commonwealth offences in the *Criminal Code;* general provisions in Chapter 7 of the *Corporations Act 2001* (Cth) (the '*Corporations Act*') concerning financial services and markets; and specific provisions in the *Corporations Act* relating to insider trading. While some States and Territories of Australia have chosen to enact their own criminal codes, the Australian Capital Territory,[37] the Northern Territory,[38] Queensland,[39] Tasmania[40] and Western Australia,[41] none has enacted statutory provisions concerning corporate criminal liability, so they all rely on the application of common law principles of vicarious liability and direct liability through the identification doctrine.

The Criminal Code

For criminal offences existing under Commonwealth laws, the *Criminal Code* operates to 'codify the general principles of criminal responsibility'.[42] Accordingly, it excludes common law rules concerning corporate criminal liability from application to the Commonwealth criminal offences to which the code applies.[43]

Instead of using the general terminology of 'actus reus' and 'mens rea', the *Criminal Code* provides that offences consist generally of 'physical elements' and 'fault elements'.[44] The *Criminal Code* describes a variety of matters that may amount

---

36 *Attorney-Generals' Reference (No 2 of 1999)* [2000] QB 796; Eilis Ferran, 'Corporate Attribution and the Directing Mind and Will' (2011) 127 *Law Quarterly Review* 239 at 246.

37 *Criminal Code 2002* (ACT).

38 *Criminal Code Act 1983* (NT).

39 *Criminal Code Act 1899* (Qld).

40 *Criminal Code Act 1924* (Tas).

41 *Criminal Code Act 1913* (WA).

42 *Criminal Code,* s. 2.1.

43 Stephen Odgers, *Principles of Federal Criminal Law* (Thomson Lawbook Co, 2007) at 7.

44 *Criminal Code,* s. 3.1(1). Despite the use of different terminology, in *The Queen v LK* [2010] HCA 17, French J. of the High Court approved a statement that the drafting of the *Criminal Code* adopted 'the usual analytical division of criminal offences into the actus reus and the mens rea or physical elements and fault elements' at [42].

to a fault element – intention, knowledge, recklessness or negligence.[45] A physical element may be conduct, a result of conduct, or a circumstance in which conduct, or a result of conduct, occurs.[46]

Part 2.5 of the *Criminal Code* also sets out general principles for establishing corporate criminal responsibility for Commonwealth offences, and provides specific rules for determining when a physical element and a fault element can be attributed to a corporation.

Section 12.2 of the *Criminal Code* provides:

> If a physical element of an offence is committed by an employee, agent or officer of a body corporate acting within the actual or apparent scope of his or her employment, or within his or her actual or apparent authority, the physical element must also be attributed to the body corporate.

The notion of an employee carrying out activities within the scope of employment is also relevant for vicarious liability, but here the *Criminal Code* extends this concept to agents and officers of a corporation acting within the scope of their authority. When assessing whether an act is done within the scope of authority, actual or apparent, common law agency principles will be relevant. It will be necessary to establish that the person either had: (i) express actual authority,[47] (ii) implied actual authority,[48] or (iii) apparent authority,[49] to engage in that activity.

Section 12.3(1) of the *Criminal Code* provides that a fault element must be attributed to a corporation that expressly, tacitly or impliedly authorises or permits the commission of an offence. Pursuant to s. 12.3(2), such an authorisation or permission may be established by:

(a) proving that the body corporate's board of directors intentionally, knowingly or recklessly carried out the relevant conduct, or expressly, tacitly or impliedly authorised or permitted the commission of the offence; or

(b) proving that a high managerial agent of the body corporate intentionally, knowingly or recklessly engaged in the relevant conduct, or expressly, tacitly or impliedly authorised or permitted the commission of the offence; or

(c) proving that a corporate culture existed within the body corporate that directed, encouraged, tolerated or led to non-compliance with the relevant provision; or

---

45 *Criminal Code*, s. 5.1.

46 *Criminal Code*, s. 4.1(1).

47 As described in *Freeman & Lockyer v Buckhurst Park Properties (Mangal) Ltd* [1964] 2 QB 480 at 502.

48 As described in *Hely-Hutchinson v Brayhead Ltd* [1968] 1 QB 549 at 583.

49 As described in *Crabtree-Vickers v Australian Direct Mail* (1975) 33 CLR 72.

(d) proving that the body corporate failed to create and maintain a corporate culture that required compliance with the relevant provision.

The board of directors of a corporation referred to in s. 12.3(2)(a) would, in certain circumstances, be regarded as the directing mind and will of a corporation in accordance with Lord Reid's pronouncements in *Tesco's case*, as would the high managerial agent in s. 12.3(2)(b).[50] However, the reference to 'corporate culture' in s. 12.3(2)(c) and (d) of the *Criminal Code* is a significant departure from common law concepts.[51] 'Corporate culture' is defined in s. 12.3(6) as:

> an attitude, policy, rule, course of conduct or practice existing within the body corporate generally or in the part of the body corporate in which the relevant activities take place.

Fisse has stated that 'corporate policy is the corporate equivalent of intention and a corporation that conducts itself with an express or implied policy of non-compliance with a criminal prohibition exhibits corporate criminal intentionality'.[52] The Model Criminal Code Officers Committee has commented further that 'it is both fair and practical to hold companies liable for the policies and practices adopted as their method of operation.'[53] However, as the provisions concerning corporate culture remain untested judicially, the scope of their application remains uncertain and, as will be discussed below, various difficulties will exist if seeking to impose criminal liability on a corporation as a consequence of its culture.

Chapter 7 of the Corporations Act

Certain Commonwealth statutes restrict the application of the attribution rules contained within the *Criminal Code*. For example, the *Corporations Act* provides that Part 2.5 of the *Criminal Code* does not apply to any offences created under Chapter 7,[54] and a separate regime for corporate criminal liability for those offences is set out in s. 769B.

For offences created under Chapter 7 of the *Corporations Act*, which concerns financial services and markets, s. 769B(1) provides that conduct engaged in on behalf of a body corporate (which will usually be relevant to the physical element of a criminal offence):

---

50 A 'high managerial agent' is defined as 'an employee, agent or officer of the body corporate with duties of such responsibility that his or her conduct may fairly be assumed to represent the body corporate's policy': *Criminal Code*, s. 12.3(6).

51 Odgers, above n43 at 187.

52 Brent Fisse, *Howard's Criminal Law* (5th edition, Law Book Company, 1990) at 606.

53 Model Criminal Code Officers Committee, *Model Criminal Code Chapters 1 and 2 – General Principles of Criminal Responsibility Report* (AGPS, December 1992) at 109.

54 *Corporations Act*, s. 769A.

(a) by a director, employee or agent of the body, within the scope of the person's actual or apparent authority; or

(b) by any other person at the direction or with the consent or agreement (whether express or implied) of a director, employee or agent of the body, where the giving of the direction, consent or agreement is within the scope of the actual or apparent authority of the director, employee or agent;

is taken for the purposes of a provision of this Chapter, or a proceeding under this Chapter, to have been engaged in also by the body corporate.

Similar provisions are contained in s. 78(2) of the *Occupational Health and Safety (Commonwealth Employment) Act 1991* (Cth), s. 8ZD of the *Taxation Administration Act 1953* (Cth), s. 84(2) of the *Competition and Consumer Act* (Cth) and s. 12GH(2) of the *Australian Securities and Investments Commission Act 2001* (Cth).

The conduct caught by s. 769B(1) goes further than that which would be caught by s. 12.2 of the *Criminal Code*, as it includes conduct engaged in by a person at the direction or with the consent or agreement of a director, employee or agent, even if it is *not* within the scope of the first person's authority.

Where it is necessary to establish the state of mind of a body corporate, which will usually be relevant to fault elements, s. 769B(3) of the *Corporations Act* provides that:

> If, in a proceeding under this Chapter in respect of conduct engaged in by a body corporate, it is necessary to establish the state of mind of the body, it is sufficient to show that a director, employee or agent of the body [corporate], being a director, employee or agent by whom the conduct was engaged in within the scope of the person's actual or apparent authority, had that state of mind.

Again, similar provisions are contained in s. 8ZD of the *Taxation Administration Act 1953* (Cth); s. 78(1) of the *Occupational Health and Safety (Commonwealth Employment) Act 1991* (Cth); s. 84(1) of the *Competition and Consumer Act 2010* (Cth) and s. 12GH(1) of the *Australian Securities and Investments Commission Act 2001* (Cth).

Unlike the *Criminal Code*, which provides a variety of means by which a fault element may be attributed to a corporation, s. 769B(3) is limited to demonstrating that the relevant director, employee or agent who engaged in the relevant conduct had the necessary state of mind to satisfy the fault element. Concepts of corporate fault are not relevant in this context.

Division 3 of Part 7.10 of the Corporations Act – Insider Trading

In Division 3 of Part 7.10 of the *Corporations Act,* which contains the insider trading prohibition, there are additional means of establishing a corporation's possession of information and knowledge, which may be relevant for both the physical and fault elements of the insider trading offence. Section 1042G(1) of the *Corporations Act* states that:

(a) a body corporate is taken to possess any information which an officer of the body corporate possesses and which came into his or her possession in the course of the performance of duties as such an officer; and

(b) if an officer of a body corporate knows any matter or thing because he or she is an officer of the body corporate, it is to be presumed that the body corporate knows the matter or thing.

Section 1042G(2) also specifically states that 'this section does not limit the application of section 769B in relation to this Division.' However, the Chapter 7 exclusion of the provisions of the *Criminal Code* continues to apply to Division 3 of Part 7.10, due to the operation of s 769A.

The possession of inside information is a physical element of the insider trading offence.[55] However, as it relates to the 'awareness' of information,[56] it concerns the 'state of mind' of the relevant person, rather than their conduct, so it supplements the provisions of s. 769B(3) discussed above.[57] The additional manner of demonstrating the possession of information by a corporation under s. 1042G(1) is restricted to information possessed by an officer, rather than an employee or an agent, and is linked to the performance of the relevant officer's duties, rather than requiring that it be within the scope of authority of the relevant director, employee or agent.

Knowledge that certain information is inside information is the fault element of the insider trading offence.[58] The provisions in s. 1042G(1)(b) of the *Corporations Act*, setting out when a body corporate is taken to know a matter or thing, appear to be applicable to this fault element. However, a requirement that the relevant officer know a matter or thing which relates to the 'quality' of information *because* he or she is an officer of a body corporate is a difficult concept to apply. Again, since the possession of information requires awareness, this method of attribution is likely to be more applicable to the physical element of the insider trading offence.

---

55 *Corporations Act,* s. 1043A(3)(1).

56 *R v Hannes* (2000) 158 FLR 359 at 398 (Spigelman CJ).

57 For a more detailed discussion, see Juliette Overland, 'The Possession and Materiality of Information in Insider Trading Cases' (2014) 32 *Company and Securities Law Journal* 353, and Juliette Overland, 'Re-evaluating the elements of the insider trading offence: Should there be a requirement for the possession of inside information?' (2016) 44 *Australian Business Law Review* 256.

58 *Corporations Act,* s 1043A(3)(1).

Difficulties and Challenges

The current models of corporate criminal liability, under both the common law and statute, are subject to a variety of criticisms, and present a number of challenges in their practical application.

Vicarious criminal liability is often criticised because a corporation can be liable for the criminal acts of junior employees in circumstances in which the corporation derives no benefit from the relevant acts and, in very large organisations, there can be great difficulty in closely supervising every employee.[59]

The 'directing mind and will' approach has been widely criticised because it restricts liability to the conduct or fault of directors and high-level managers.[60] This favours larger corporations which will escape liability for acts of most employees,[61] encouraging delegation to more junior staff, and because criminal liability may be avoided by retaining an ultimate discretion within the board.[62]

Although the provisions of the *Criminal Code* concerning corporate criminal liability do not apply to offences in Part 7 of the *Corporations Act,* the *Corporations Act* does not exclude the common law or provide that the statutory mechanisms in Part 7 are to be exclusive. This means that, for example, for offences such as insider trading, in addition to the rules contained in s. 769B and s. 1042G of the *Corporations Act,* the common law identification doctrine may also be available to attribute criminal liability to corporations. This creates multiple possible mechanisms of attributing this criminal offence to a corporation, which leads to possible confusion as to the circumstances in which a corporation will have criminal liability.

With different rules of attribution applying under the laws of each State and Territory, and under Commonwealth laws, as well as under various pieces of legislation, confusion as to the circumstances in which a corporation will have criminal liability is exacerbated. Since a variety of mechanisms are available to attribute fault elements and physical elements, or actus reus and mens rea, to corporations, it is difficult for a corporation to be certain of the manner in which this may occur for different offences. This is particularly problematic for corporations undertaking business activities nationally and internationally. Some mechanisms of attribution will only apply where the relevant conduct occurs within the scope of a person's employment or authority. Some require a nexus with the person's role and responsibilities. Some

---

59 See, for example, James Gobert, 'Corporate Criminality: Four Models of Fault' (1994) 14 *Legal Studies* 393 at 398.

60 Fisse, above n1; Ferran, above n36 at 242.

61 Gobert, above n59 at 400; Eric Colvin, 'Corporate Personality and Criminal Liability' (1995) 6 *Criminal Law Forum* 1 at 15.

62 Jennifer Hill and Ronald Harmer, 'Criminal Liability of Corporations – Australia' in De Doelder and Tiedemann (eds), *Criminal Liability of Corporations* (Kluwer Law International, 1994) 71 at 81–2.

only apply where the person holds a position of seniority within the corporation, whereas others extend to employees and agents. While different forms of criminal conduct may necessarily require mechanisms of attribution that are appropriately tailored to the relevant offence, the overlap and resulting confusion between the various mechanisms which may apply must be acknowledged.

The uncertainty which can exist in determining whether or not certain physical or fault elements may be attributed to a corporation was illustrated by *ASIC v Citigroup Global Markets Australia Pty Ltd*[63] (*Citigroup's case*). In that case, a set of civil penalty proceedings for insider trading, it was necessary to determine whether a proprietary trader employed by Citigroup possessed certain information, and whether the possession of that information was to be attributed to Citigroup. Jacobson J. of the Federal Court determined that even if the proprietary trader had possessed the relevant information, it was not possessed by Citigroup under s. 1042G(1)(a) because he was not an 'officer' of the corporation as defined in section 9 of the *Corporations Act*. He was one of five proprietary traders employed by Citigroup and had no employees reporting to him and no other responsibilities aside from proprietary trading. The fact that he had a daily trading limit of $10 million did not 'make him a person who had the capacity to affect Citigroup's financial standing', as this was not a significant sum 'in the context of Citigroup's very substantial business.' Additionally, as a proprietary trader, Mr Manchee did not have 'any involvement in policy making or decisions that affected the whole or a substantial part of the business of Citigroup'.[64]

One can infer from the judgment in *Citigroup's case* that the Court was not presented with arguments concerning alternative means of attributing the possession of information to a corporation, since it appears that ASIC assumed that the proprietary trader would be regarded as an officer of Citigroup and that s. 1042G(1)(a) would therefore apply.[65] If regulators have difficulty in determining when and how attribution provisions are to be applied, this not only indicates the similar difficulties that corporations face, but also highlights the problems that exist in the effective enforcement of criminal and civil breaches by corporations.

Developments and Current Trends

There has been a resurgence of interest in the potential use of 'corporate culture' as a means of attributing corporate criminal liability, particularly in connection with financial institutions. In the aftermath of the Global Financial Crisis, banking

---

63 (2007) 160 FCR 35.

64 Ibid at 99.

65 Ibid at 99–101; Ashley Black, 'Insider Trading and Market Misconduct' (2011) 29 *Company and Securities Law Journal* 313 at 320.

culture and lending practices were subject to significant criticism.[66] Indeed, ASIC has noted that '[p]oor culture, resulting in lack of transparency and chronic under-pricing of risk, has been noted as one of the causes of the 2008 global financial crisis and remains a risk.'[67] More recently, ASIC has indicated that it intends to increase its focus on corporate culture in the banking and financial services industries,[68] accompanied by a Royal Commission into the banking industry.[69] In particular, ASIC has stated that it considers that 'cultural factors in … banking and financial services institutions … may have contributed to [various] systemic failures', especially failures concerning the giving of financial advice.[70] Former ASIC Chair, Greg Medcraft, has also stated that 'culture matters to ASIC because poor culture can be a driver to poor conduct. Culture has been at the root of some of the worst misconduct we've seen in the financial sector.'[71]

Despite this renewed focus on corporate culture as a means of indicating culpability of organisations, the provisions concerning corporate culture under the *Criminal Code* are as yet untested, as noted above, so the true scope of their possible application remains uncertain. There are, however, many criticisms of these attempts to use corporate culture as a means of attributing corporate criminal liability in the financial sector.[72] Additionally, Chapter 7 of the *Corporations Act,* which regulates financial services and markets, excludes the operation of the Criminal Code by virtue of the provisions of s. 769A. This makes the provisions of Part 2.5 of the

---

66 Michael Legg and Jason Harris, 'How the American Dream became a Global Night-mare' (2009) 32 *University of New South Wales Law Journal* 350 at 367.

67 ASIC, Corporate Plan 2015–2016 to 2018–2019 at 6: <http://asic.gov.au/about-asic/what-we-do/our-role/asics-corporate-plan-2015-2016-to-2018-2019/>.

68 See, for example, former ASIC Chair Greg Medcraft, 'The Importance of Corporate Culture', speech given at the Gilbert & Tobin Board Luncheon (15 June 2017); former ASIC Chair Greg Medcraft, 'The Importance of Corporate Culture', speech given at AHRI Senior HR Leaders Forum Luncheon (5 April 2017); ASIC Commissioner John Price, 'The Current State of Corporate Culture', speech given at the Governance Institute of Australia, 33rd National Conference (28 November 2016); ASIC Commissioner Cathie Armour, 'Regulatory Perspective on Conduct, Risk, Culture and Governance' speech given at the Risk Australia Conference (18 August 2016); 'ASIC tells banks to raise bar on corporate culture', *Australian* (21 July 2016); 'ASIC tells investment banks corporate culture shift "needs to happen now"', *Sydney Morning Herald* (27 May 2015); 'Banking culture at heart of ASIC suit', *Australian Financial Review* (7 March 2016).

69 See, for example, 'Coalition split on banking royal commission as Malcolm Turnbull faces flak over "captain's call"', *Sydney Morning Herald* (11 April 2016); 'Shorten's push for banking royal commission makes sense', *Australian* (1 April 2017).

70 ASIC, Report 499, *Financial Advice: Fees for No Service* (October 2016) at 42.

71 Former ASIC Chair, Greg Medcraft, 'Corporate Culture and Corporate Regulation', Speech given to the Business Law Section of the Law Council of Australia (20 November 2015).

72 See, for example, John Colvin and James Argent, 'Corporate and personal liability for 'culture' in organisations' (2016) 34 *Company and Securities Law Journal* 30.

Criminal Code, providing for corporate criminal liability through corporate culture amongst other mechanisms, inapplicable – although ASIC has recommended that the *Corporations Act* be amended to remove this impediment. Accordingly, Tomasic concludes that 'the existence of inadequate corporate culture is unlikely to be an effective means of proving criminal misconduct in financial institutions.'[73] Regardless, Dixon notes that a key difficulty would arise in applying the provisions concerning corporate culture in that it would involve 'the onerous task of proving that culture. One of the primary difficulties is that the culture must relate to the physical act and be evidenced at the point in time that the physical act took place.'[74] Colvin and Argent also note the extreme difficulty of attempting to 'define and measure culture for the purposes of imposing legal liability.'[75]

Thus it can be seen that, within Australia at least, the attribution of criminal liability to corporations remains fraught. The various different mechanisms that exist, of which a number are untested, cause significant uncertainty in this context. The availability and overlap between the different mechanisms of attribution makes it difficult to definitively state which mechanism will operate or the manner in which it should apply. Corporations, and those who work within them, deserve to be afforded greater certainty as to when the organisation is likely to be the subject of corporate criminal liability. Similarly, regulators, who are often the subject of criticism for the lack of enforcement action or a lack of success in actions brought, are hampered in their roles without sufficient clarity as to when organisations they may pursue are likely to be found to have engaged in criminal conduct.

---

73 Roman Tomasic, 'Exploring the Limits of Corporate Culture as a Regulatory Tool in Legalistic Corporate Law Settings – The Case of Financial Institutions', *Corporate Law Teachers Association Conference* (6 February 2017).

74 Olivia Dixon, 'Corporate Criminal Liability: The Influence of Corporate Culture' in *Integrity, Risk and Accountability in Capital Markets – Regulating Culture*, by O'Brien and Gilligan (eds) (Hart Publishing, 2013) 267.

75 Colvin and Argent, above n72 at 47.

Chapter 5

Recent Peeks under the Corporate Veil

David Bennett AC QC

I start with Gilbert and Sullivan. For a lawyer, their best operetta is not Trial by Jury but Utopia Limited. Unfortunately it is rarely performed because it is the only one of their works requiring a full change of costume by the female chorus. This makes it expensive. The operetta is of interest to both constitutional lawyers and company lawyers.

The constitutional aspect concerns the constitution of the island kingdom of Utopia before the changes it described. It is ruled by a king who has absolute powers except in one respect. There are two 'wise men' who, if he becomes too despotic, have only one constitutional power – to instruct an officer, called the Royal Exploder, to blow up the king with dynamite. This could be described as the ultimate system of checks and balances. It may bear some resemblance to the effect of our reserve powers, although, of course, Gilbert and Sullivan would never have heard of them. It also bears some resemblance to the theory of corporate governance which provides that the only function of the board should be to hire and fire the chief executive.

The King decides that England is doing better than Utopia so he decides to reform it by importing six men who represent between them what has made Britain great (the six flowers of progress). They are Captain Fitzbattleaxe, a grenadier guard, Captain Sir Edward Corcoran KCB RN, Lord Dramaleigh, a lord chamberlain, Mr Blushington, a county councillor, a barrister called Sir Bailey Barre QC MP and, most importantly for our purposes, a company promoter called Mr Goldbury. This was, of course, immediately after *Salomon* v *Salomon & Co*,[1] and there was no doubt a tinge of anti-Semitism in the nomenclature. Mr Goldbury sings one song extolling the virtues of corporate limited liability. Let me quote it for you:[2]

> Some seven men form an Association
> (If possible, all Peers and Baronets)
> They start off with a public declaration
> To what extent they mean to pay their debts.
> That's called their Capital; if they are wary
> They will not quote it at a sum immense.
> The figure's immaterial – it may vary
> From eighteen million down to eighteenpence.

1 *Salomon v Salomon & Co Ltd* [1897] AC 22.
2 Gilbert and Sullivan Archive: Utopia Limited.

I should put it rather low;
The good sense of doing so
Will be evident at once to any debtor.
When it's left to you to say
What amount you mean to pay,
Why, the lower you can put it at, the better.

They then proceed to trade with all who'll trust 'em,
Quite irrespective of their capital
(It's shady, but it's sanctified by custom);
Bank, Railway, Loan, or Panama Canal.
You can't embark on trading too tremendous –
It's strictly fair, and based on common sense –
If you succeed, your profits are stupendous –
And if you fail, pop goes your eighteenpence.

...

If you come to grief, and creditors are craving,
(For nothing that is planned by mortal head
Is certain in this Vale of Sorrow – saving
That one's Liability is Limited), –
Do you suppose that signifies perdition?
If so you're but a monetary dunce –
You merely file a Winding-Up Petition,
And start another company at once!
Though a Rothschild you may be
In your own capacity,
As a Company you've come to utter sorrow –
But the liquidators say,
'Never mind – you needn't pay,'
So you start another company to-morrow!

He then proceeds to re-organise the country on corporate lines. Its name is changed to Utopia Limited and every child on being born becomes a limited liability company.

The operetta has a happy ending because the wise men realise that one cannot blow up a limited company, as the king now is, and therefore they have become powerless.

Since the late nineteenth century, limited liability has been a given, although there are still some left-leaning academics who do not like it.[3] There have been two recent UK cases in which the veil has been lifted in the Mareva injunction context. In *Atlas v Avalon (No. 3)*,[4] the court refused the usual allowance to the defendant company where its holding company had available assets. In *TSB Private Bank v*

---

3 See the useful article by Helen Anderson, 'Piercing the Veil on Corporate Groups in Australia: the Case for Reform' (2009) 33(2) *MULR* 333.

4 *Atlas v Avalon (No 3)* [1991] 4 All ER 783.

Chabra,[5] a Mareva injunction was granted against a company which was 'the alter ego' (whatever that means) of an insolvent defendant.

In Australia, in *CSR v Wren*,[6] it was held that a holding company may be liable for negligent failure to supervise a negligent subsidiary. This was in an asbestos context, and there is little else to justify it. Absent special considerations, Australian courts have held the line against granting asbestos plaintiffs access to holding companies,[7] while in the United States, the corporate veil is lifted to give tort plaintiffs access to the holding companies of totally controlled defendant subsidiaries.[8] The US cases go much further than the common law rule.

Old-fashioned lawyers like myself still consider that there is something vaguely indecent about peeking underneath the corporate veil. We believe, as an article of faith, that *Salomon v. Salomon & Co. Ltd*[9] laid down for all time one of the basic principles of the common law. Those who seek to avoid it or peer beneath it are at best iconoclasts and at worst perverts.

Judges in general seem to be talking more about lifting the corporate veil but doing it less. Certainly there are modern cases where it has been lifted. On analysis, however, most are comparatively uncontroversial and the small number of cases where there has been a genuine lifting of the veil can easily be dismissed as being simply wrong.

I should add that I am not concerned at all in this chapter with statutory lifting of the veil. Tests for controls such as those laid down in the takeovers code do not involve any lifting of the corporate veil – they merely involve statutory interpretation. My concern is with cases where it has been suggested that judges should simply ignore the existence of a corporation so as to achieve what is erroneously perceived to be a just result.

Criminal Law

This is an area where there must be a particularly great temptation to ignore the corporate veil. In fact, the modern decisions suggest that the veil will be lifted in favour of an accused person but not in favour of the prosecution.

In *R v Roffel*,[10] a husband and wife were the sole directors and shareholders of a family company. The husband drew cheques on the company payable to himself and was charged with theft. It was held that, as he was the directing mind and will of the company and had consented to the transactions, no theft had occurred. The case is

5 *TSB Private Bank v Chabra* [1992] 2 All ER 245.

6 *CSR v Wren* (1998) 44 NSWLR 463.

7 See for example, *James Hardie & Co Ltd v Hall* (1998) 43 NSWLR 554.

8 See for example, *Craig v Lake Asbestos of Quebec* 843 F 2d 145 (3d Cir. 1988).

9 Above n1.

10 *R v Roffel* [1985] VR 511.

not really a case on the corporate veil as such, but it is interesting to note that the Full Court of Queensland expressed some doubt about the decision in *R v Maher*.[11] That case involved a conspiracy to defraud a company of its assets and one can understand a different view being taken.

There are a number of cases in which an issue more closely related to the corporate veil has been considered – the question whether a crime is committed by a person in his or her capacity as an officer of a company.

In *R v. Ditford*[12] it was held that a person was not guilty of 'entering into a transaction for the purpose of securing that a company will be unable to pay its future income tax' within the meaning of the *Crimes (Taxation Offences) Act* 1980, where all the transactions entered into were transactions of a company in relation to which the accused was the only deciding party and one of the executing parties. In particular, the court rejected the Crown's submission that the accused entered into a relevant transaction merely because he resolved or determined that a company which he controlled would do so.

The decision can, perhaps, be characterised as merely one on the meaning of the words 'enters into a transaction'. It is, however, a useful rejection of what otherwise might be thought to have been woolly thinking.

Another decision which can be limited to the meaning of words is *Hamilton v. Whitehead*.[13] A company was charged with issuing a prescribed interest and its managing director, who had done all the relevant acts, was charged with being knowingly concerned. It was argued, based on *Mallon v. Lee*,[14] that a principal offender could not be liable vicariously and therefore that a director could not be charged with being knowingly concerned in his own act. This suggestion was rejected by the High Court, largely on the basis of the fact that the relevant provision appeared in the Companies Code and that the Code, on its true construction, clearly intended that the 'knowingly concerned' provisions would catch directors in this type of situation.

For the reasons I have given, none of these criminal cases really involve anything very helpful about the lifting of the corporate veil.

Damages cases where the veil is sought to be lifted in relation to the plaintiff

There are a number of situations in which a corporate plaintiff may be inhibited in relation to the damages it can recover by the existence of a corporate veil.

One of the silliest examples of this is *DHN Food Distributors Limited v. Tower*

---

11 *R v Maher* [1987] 1 Qd R 171 at 195.

12 *R v Ditford* 87 ATC 4693.

13 *Hamilton v Whitehead* (1988) 7 ACLC 34.

14 *Mallon v Lee* (1949) 80 CLR 198.

Hamlets London Borough Council.[15] In that case a council was liable to the owner under a compulsory acquisition statute for compensation for disturbance. The land was owned by a company but occupied by two wholly owned subsidiaries which suffered the relevant loss. Lord Denning put the manner in his traditional forthright and imprecise manner, stating:[16]

> This group is virtually the same as a partnership in which all the three companies are partners. They should not be treated separately so as to be defeated on a technical point. They should not be deprived of the compensation which should justly be payable for disturbance. The three companies should, for present purposes, be treated as one and the parent company DHN should be treated as that one.

The test in that case was whether there had been any disturbance of the occupation of the holding company. While the court also found for the plaintiff on issues based on implied licences and equitable interests, all members of the court mouthed extreme dicta in relation to the need to lift the corporate veil in order to deal fairly with the plaintiff's claim.

The case has been criticised in New Zealand[17] and New South Wales,[18] while the House of Lords added its disapproval in *Woolfson v. Strathclyde Regional Council,*[19] a case involving a very similar factual problem.

A related problem arose in *South Coast Basalt Pty Ltd v. R W Miller Holdings Limited.*[20] In that case the defendant, in breach of contract, caused certain aggregate belonging to the plaintiff to be contaminated with sugar while being transported in a ship. The aggregate was 'invoiced across in the books' to Pioneer Concrete (NSW) Pty Limited. Both Pioneer Concrete (NSW) Pty Limited and South Coast Basalt Pty Limited were wholly owned subsidiaries of Pioneer Concrete Services Limited. The means by which aggregate was transferred from the aggregate mining company (South Coast Basalt Pty Limited) to the trading company was by a series of debits and credits in the books of the two companies. Pioneer Concrete NSW Pty Limited then made concrete with the contaminated aggregate and sold it to third parties. When the concrete failed to set it suffered substantial losses. The trial judge (Yeldham J.) held that those losses could not be recovered. The Privy Council, however, held that the warranties implied by the *Sale of Goods Act* applied to the 'invoicing across' of the aggregate and therefore that the plaintiff had suffered a loss because it had incurred

---

15 *DHN Food Distributors Limited v Tower Hamlets London Borough Council* [1976] 1 WLR 852.

16 Id at 860. A similar position was taken by Goff and Shaw L.J.J.

17 *Re Securitibank Ltd* [1978] 1 NZLR 97 at 133.

18 *Pioneer Concrete Services Ltd v. Yelnah Pty Ltd* (1986) 5 NSWLR 254 at 266.

19 *Woolfson v. Strathclyde Regional Council* [1978] P & CR 521.

20 [1979] UKPC 39

a liability to its co-subsidiary. The Privy Council was unmoved by the argument that the co-subsidiary would be highly unlikely to sue, except perhaps for the purpose of creating a liability in the third party. The result was in accordance with common sense and did not involve any lifting of the corporate veil.

The interesting thing about this case is that both sides could claim to be seeking to lift the veil. The plaintiff wished to recover for the benefit of one company a loss suffered by a related company. The defendant wished to ignore the contract for sale of goods between the two related companies – or at least treat it as different from a sale of goods between unrelated parties. In the result, no veil was lifted at all and justice was done.

In *Concrete Systems Pty Ltd v. Devon Symonds Holdings Limited*,[21] Sangster J. made some comments in obiter to the effect that where one company in a group owned copyright in plans and was recovering damages for infringement and another company in the group (the builder) was the one which would have obtained the profits from the use of the copyright, those losses could not be recovered. His Honour concluded by saying:[22]

> In my opinion, if a proprietor chooses to operate by means of a group of companies (obviously for some purpose advantageous to himself) he cannot complain if the means chosen by him to derive such a purpose deprives him of some other advantage which he might otherwise have had – such as, in this case, damages for loss of profit on building and selling houses, and not merely damages for allowing, for a fee, the use of plans.

The High Court itself made some comments on this problem in *Gould v. Vaggelas*.[23] In that case misrepresentations were made to individuals who, in reliance upon the representations, formed a company and caused it to purchase property. The representations were fraudulent and the property was worth less than was paid for it. The individuals sued and recovered damages. It was held that there was no obligation upon them to cause the company to sue and take the damages it could have recovered. Wilson J. commented that, if the company recovered damages, the individuals would not be entitled to recover damages against the company without giving credit for what they had received. The real problem of overlap between the damages the company was likely to recover and damages recovered by the individuals was not seriously addressed. Gibbs C.J., for example, said:[24]

> I should add that if Gould Holdings were to proceed with its action, the question might arise, first, whether the Goulds, having been fully

---

21 *Concrete Systems Pty Ltd v Devon Symonds Holdings Limited* (1979) 47 FLR 1.

22 Id at 14 .The *DHN case* was not cited.

23 *Gould v Veggelas* (1983–5) 157 CLR 215.

24 Id at 229.

compensated for the loss which they suffered in making the advances on the company's behalf, could then recover the amount of those advances from the company and, if they could recover, whether any of the respondents would be subrogated to their rights and, secondly, if they could not recover from the company, whether this would reduce the company's consequential loss, and thus the quantum of the damages to which it might be entitled. In any case, as I have already indicated, the fact that the company might have rights against the respondents does not mean that the Goulds are precluded from enforcing their own personal rights.

While one welcomes the refusal to lift the corporate veil, this approach does have some problems. Assume that a vendor represents to individuals, fraudulently, that a property has characteristics it does not have. The individuals form a company and cause it to buy the property. They subscribe $1 million for this purpose and the company pays $1 million for a property worth $500,000. Assume further that the representations are repeated to the company after incorporation and before contract and that the individuals relied on the representations to form the company and lend it $1 million and the company relied on the representations to buy the property. The problem in reality is not so much one of lifting the corporate veil as one of determining precisely what damage the individuals and the company have suffered. If the company recovers damages in full, the individuals have suffered no damage. If, however, the individuals sue first and recover damages, one needs, presumably, to place some value on the company's asset being its claim for damages in order to determine the damages the individuals should recover. It is this last step which appears to have been glossed over by the High Court although the facts in *Gould v. Vaggelas* were not quite as simple as those in the example I have given.

In *Prudential Assurance Co. Ltd v. Newman Industries Ltd,*[25] the Court of Appeal took the simplistic position that no damages could be recovered by a shareholder for a diminution in the value of shares through loss to a company. The example was given of a company with two shareholders – one with ninety-nine shares and one with one share. The company's sole asset is a cash box with £100,000 to which the majority shareholder has the key. The minority shareholder makes a fraudulent representation to the majority shareholder persuading him to part with the key so that the former can steal the money. The view of the Court of Appeal was that the company could sue but that the shareholder could not.

This solution may be tidy but it is not logically consistent. Suppose the circumstances are that the loss is caused to the company but that, for some reason, the company has no right of action (for example the money being used in accordance with the articles but contrary to a shareholders' agreement). A rule that diminution in value of shares is never actionable at the suit of a shareholder seems to be inconsistent with principle however well it may solve particular anomalies.

---

25 *Prudential Assurance Co Ltd v Newman Industries Ltd* [1982] Ch 204 at 223.

A more sophisticated example might occur if the individuals owned all the shares in a proprietary company, received the fraudulent misrepresentation and then, in reliance upon it, failed to take steps they otherwise would have taken. Those steps would have involved a public listing of the company, the retention of 10 per cent of the shareholding and the making of substantial profits by the company. If the company sues and obtains full damages, the individuals have received a windfall since, had the fraudulent representation not been made, they would only have benefited to the extent of 10 per cent. There is no obvious solution to this problem except perhaps that they obtain the windfall. It is a consequence of the loss being the company's loss.

Damages Cases where the Corporate Veil is sought to be lifted in relation to the defendant

It is hard to imagine circumstances in which the corporate veil should be lifted where a wrong is done by a company and the wronged party wishes to go behind the company to the perpetrator of the wrong. In *Schouls v Canadian Meat Processing Corporation*,[26] Trainor J. of the Supreme Court of Ontario was faced with a wrongful dismissal case where the dismissal had been carried out by the plaintiff and majority shareholder of a company. There was no doubt that the company was liable: the question was whether there was any cause of action against the controlling party. His Honour correctly held that there was no contractual relationship and no tort for which that person could be liable. However, and inexplicably from the point of view of Australian law, His Honour concluded:[27]

> The defendant Paletta is the sole cause of this litigation. As a consequence of his handling of the plaintiff's termination and his total disregard for the disruption and injury which he caused to the plaintiff and his family, he should be responsible in his personal capacity, together with the corporate defendant, for the plaintiff's solicitor and client costs. I so order.

More recently, in both the United States and Australia there have been attempts to sheet home liability for asbestos-related torts to holding companies. No doubt a similar exercise took place in the courts in Bhopal but I am not aware of the results of any such litigation.

In *Craig v. Johns-Manville Corporation*[28] the Court of Appeals in the 3rd Circuit refused to hold that a holding company was liable. The court applied the rule that:[29]

---

26 *Schouls v Canadian Meat Processing Corporation* (1983) [1980–84] LRC (Comm) 778.

27 Id at 783.

28 *Craig v Lake Asbestos of Quebec* 843 F 2d 145 (3d Cir 1988).

29 Id at 149.

Even in the case of a parent corporation and its wholly owned subsidiary, limited liability normally will not be abrogated ... the corporate veil may be pierced only where 1) the parent so dominated the subsidiary that it had no separate existence but was merely a conduit for the parent and 2) the parent had abused the privilege of incorporation by using the subsidiary to perpetrate a fraud or injustice or otherwise to circumvent the law.

This appears to be the current test in the United States.

A similar attempt was made in Australia in *Briggs v James Hardie & Co Pty Ltd*.[30] This was an application to strike out a joinder of two joint venturers which owned all the shares in the operating company. The application was one for an extension of time and the court held that, there being some possibility of the corporate veil being lifted, the actions ought not to be effectively struck out by a refusal of the extension. The decision is rather more an indication of the ease of obtaining an extension of time than it is of lifting the corporate veil. Meagher J.A. dissented.

So far as I can ascertain, the action against the holding companies has not been the subject of a subsequent reported decision.

Miscellaneous cases

There a number of miscellaneous cases where the courts have considered questions similar to those which have arisen in the cases I have considered.

One of the earliest decisions since *Salomon's case* is the decision of the Supreme Court of Appeals of Virginia in *People's Pleasure Park Co. Inc. v. Rohleder*.[31] That case concerned a covenant that title to certain land should never vest in a person of African descent or a coloured person. Lots were conveyed to a corporation all of whose shareholders were Negroes which was established for the purpose of establishing an amusement park for coloured people. The case was decided, of course, in the absence of modern concepts of discrimination law and there was no serious question about the validity of the covenant. The court held that the corporate veil could not be lifted and accordingly that there was no breach of covenant.

There have been attempts to argue the significance of lifting the corporate veil in cases where the real issues are discretionary. Thus in *re Hanamoa Pty Ltd*,[32] a company sought to resist a winding up order on the basis that, although the petitioner wife had established all the necessary elements, the company was 'in reality' a vehicle for the husband and wife to carry on their business operations and that the court should not treat it as a normal company. Not surprisingly this submission failed.

In *Atlas Maritime Co. SA v. Avalon Maritime Limited (No. 3)*[33] the English

---

30 *Briggs v James Hardie & Co Pty Ltd* (1989) 16 NSWLR 549.

31 *People's Pleasure Park C. Inc v Rohleder* (1908) 61 SE 794.

32 *Re Hanamoa Pty Ltd* (1982) 7 ACLR 30.

33 *Atlas Maritime Co. SA v Avalon Maritime Limited (No. 3)* [1991] 1 WLR 917.

Court of Appeal refused to allow a subsidiary which was the subject of a Mareva injunction to obtain a release of funds to pay its costs on the basis that those costs could be paid by its holding company. The court took the view that the issue was one of discretion and that the corporate veil played no part in exercising such a discretion.

This approach was taken further by Mummery J. in *TSB Private Bank International SA v. Chabra*.[34] The court granted a Mareva injunction against a related company on the ground that there was a good arguable case that assets apparently vested in the name of BHL were in fact beneficially the property of the first defendant and that BHL was, at the relevant time, the alter ego of the first defendant and therefore its assets, or at least some of its assets, might be available to satisfy claims against the first defendant.[35]

The first and third of these matters may well be proper discretionary bases for a Mareva injunction. I have my doubts about the second unless it is treated as nothing more than an evidentiary fact leading to the third.

It should be noted that, contrary to popular superstition, the mere fact that a case involves taxation is insufficient justification for a lifting of the corporate veil.[36]

An illustration of the extreme reluctance of the courts to lift the corporate veil appears in *Creasey v. Breachwood Motors Limited*.[37] In that case a company took over all the assets of another company and paid all its liabilities except one. The original debtor company was then dissolved. The one remaining creditor sued the new company. It was argued that there was a general presumption in law that where the whole of the assets of a company were taken over by a different company, liabilities were transferred as well as assets; alternatively that the court should lift the corporate veil and not let the acquiring company obtain the benefit of the business but leave a claim unpaid. Southwell QC, sitting as an acting judge of the Queen's Bench Division, held that there was no authority for the proposition contended for and that the corporate veil would not be lifted.

In *Prest v Petrodel Resources Ltd*,[38] the Supreme Court of the United Kingdom allowed an appeal from a decision in a matrimonial case in which the trial judge had lifted the corporate veil and ordered the husband to 'procure' the transfer to the wife of the assets of a company which he controlled. The case contains a useful analysis of many of the cases on lifting the corporate veil. Of course many orders made in matrimonial cases involve achieving the result that assets transferred by one party to a company be made available to the other but this can usually be achieved without

---

34 *TSB Private Bank International SA v Chabra* [1992] 1 WLR 231.

35 Id at 238.

36 See *Dennis Willcox Pty Ltd v Federal Commissioner of Taxation* (1988) 79 ALR 267.

37 See *Creasey v Breachwood Motors Limited* (1992) 10 ACLC 3052.

38 *Prest v Petrodel Resources Ltd* [2013] UKSC 34.

any lifting of the corporate veil. There is a further detailed analysis of the doctrine and its history by the same court in *VTB Capital plc v Nutritek Corp.*[39] Both cases reject the idea that there is any general doctrine under which the corporate veil may be lifted.

Conclusions

Increasingly in the law there are situations in which it might appear to be desirable to lift the corporate veil in order to do what appears to be rough justice between the parties. To date, with one or two very minor exceptions, the courts have valiantly held the line and resisted the temptation to succumb to the blandishments of those who would wish such an approach to be taken. It is to be hoped that this sensible approach will continue.

I conclude by saying that I do not understand why one would describe the activity as 'piercing' the veil. Piercing a veil, is quite pointless because it does not reveal anything. I prefer the metaphor of lifting the veil – something which conjures up a rather more attractive image.

---

39 See *VTB Capital plc v Nutritek Corp* [2013] UKSC 5.

Chapter 6

Who has the control of Alibaba Group? Piercing the Unorthodox Corporate Structure of the E-Commerce Giant

Zhaozhao Wu

On 19 September 2014, Alibaba Group Holding Limited (Alibaba Group) netted US$25 billion on the New York Stock Exchange (NYSE), making it the biggest Initial Public Offering (IPO) in the world.[1]

It is also one of the most volatile stocks on the market. Within one year of the IPO, Alibaba's shares tumbled nearly 30 per cent shaving off approximately US$140 billion from the company's market value.[2] In the fiscal year of 2017, Alibaba's shares have nearly doubled, racing Amazon to the US$500 billion goal.[3]

The legendary achievements of the company so far are only made possible because: (a) under the United States (US) General Accepted Accounting Principles, the revenues generated by a Chinese Variable Interest Entity (VIE) in which Alibaba Group holds the controlling interest through a non-ownership legal arrangement is recognised as part of the consolidated revenue; and (b) the stock exchanges in US allows for dual-class shares with different weighted voting rights to be issued by a listed company. VIE and Alibaba Partnership[4] are the two pillars of the unorthodox corporate structure of the Alibaba Group that is made of 630 subsidiaries and other consolidated entities.[5] The opaque corporate structure receives skepticism from

---

1 Ryan Mac, 'Alibaba Claims Title for Largest Global IPO Ever with Extra Share Sales', *Forbes* (22 September 2014): <http://www.forbes.com/sites/ryanmac/2014/09/22/alibaba-claims-title-for-largest-global-ipo-ever-with-extra-share-sales/>.

2 Akin Oyedele, 'Happy 1-year anniversary, Alibaba!', *Business Insider Australia* (18 September 2015): <https://www.businessinsider.com.au/alibaba-one-year-since-ipo-2015-9?r=US&IR=T>.

3 Deirdre Bosa, 'Alibaba vs Amazon: The race to $500 billion', *CNBC* (1 September 2017): <https://www.cnbc.com/2017/09/01/alibaba-vs-amazon-the-race-to-500-billion.html>.

4 The dual-class shares are referred to in the prospectus for Alibaba Group's IPO. See more in Amendment No. 3 to Form F-1 Registration statement under the Securities Act of 1933 (11 July 2014): <https://www.sec.gov/Archives/edgar/data/1577552/000119312514266462/d709111df1a.htm>.

5 Alibaba Group Holding Limited, Annual Report pursuant to Section 13 or 15(D) of the Securities Exchange Act of 1934. For the fiscal year ended 31 March 2017: < http://otp.in-vestis.com/clients/us/alibaba/SEC/sec-show.aspx?FilingId=12129538&Cik=0001577552&-

investors, analysts and regulators: challenging Alibaba's corporate governance.

This chapter reviews the unique features of Alibaba Group's corporate structure, identifies the legal risks of such an unorthodox corporate structure and explores the options to enhance the accountability of its management.

Variable Interest Entity

Chinese companies in the internet industry have a long history of adopting a VIE structure. In 2000, SINA Corporation, a Chinese online-media company, first used a VIE structure to obtain a listing on Nasdaq.[6] This listing occurred three years before the Financial Accounting Standards Board promulgated Interpretation No. 46, Consolidation of Variable Interest Entities, (FIN 46), so as to curb the abuse of related entities in off-balance sheet financing as exposed in the Enron Scandal. The same FIN 46 created a novel way for Chinese companies to raise funds in the US.[7] According to the financial filings for 2013, almost half of the Chinese companies listed on either the NYSE or Nasdaq are in the form of a VIE or a variation of a VIE.[8]

The prevalence of the VIE is driven by the need to circumvent Chinese restrictions on foreign investment in certain industries such as technology, communications and education. In particular, under Chinese law, internet companies in China, including all e-commerce platforms, must apply for an internet content provider licence (ICP licence) in order to operate their websites. Chinese law restricts or prohibits a wholly foreign-owned enterprise or a domestic company with a foreign majority holding from obtaining an ICP licence.[9]

Type=PDF&hasPdf=1>.

6 Paul Gills, *The Big Four and the Development of the Accounting Profession in China (Studies in the Development of Accounting Thought)* (Emerald Group Publishing, 2014) at 137.

7 Justin Hopkins, Mark Lang and Donny Zhao, 'When Enron Met Alibaba: The Rise of VIEs in China'. Paper presented at the Research Seminar of School of Accountancy at Chinese University of Hong Kong (10 December 2016).

8 李艳娜 [Li Yanna], '新《外国投资法》下VIE模式的法律风险' [Legal Risks of VIE under the New Foreign Investment Law] (2015) 3,《中国对外贸易》[China's Foreign Trade].

9 《互联网信息服务管理办法》[Administrative Measures on Internet Information Services] 国务院 [State Council] promulgated on 25 September 2000 and amended on 8 January 2011. Specifically, foreign investors are generally not permitted to own more than 50% of shares in a company that provides value-added telecommunication services. This requirement has been relaxed by a subsequent inferior legislation promulgated by the Ministry of Industry and Information Technology on 19 June 2015 – 'Notice on Lifting the Restriction to Foreign Shareholding Percentage in Online Data Processing and Transaction Processing Business (Operational E-commerce)' – to allow foreign investors to wholly own all the shares of a company that is in the online data processing and transaction processing business (operational e-commerce) in China. However, any such foreign investor still has to demonstrate a good track record in providing value-added telecommunications services overseas. This criteria is not likely to be met by any retail or institutional investors on a capital market.

In order to acquire or keep the necessary ICP licence, an e-commerce company must establish a Chinese operation company whose shareholders are Chinese citizens. The wholly owned Chinese company will be the applicant and holder of the ICP licence. This is commonly referred to as 'OpCo' in a VIE structure. Also, a holding company will be set up to raise funds in a foreign capital market. This is commonly referred to as 'ListCo' in a VIE structure. To funnel the raised funds to China, it usually requires the establishment of a wholly foreign-owned company domiciled in China. This is commonly referred to as 'WFOE' in a VIE structure.[10] See figure 1 below. By arranging for OpCo, ListCo and WFOE to enter into a series of contracts, a VIE structure is set up to make the e-commerce company appear to be solely owned by Chinese citizens, and make foreign investors appear to be the primary beneficiaries of the VIE in accordance with the risk and rewards principle in FIN 46.[11] Thus, the VIE's revenue must be consolidated into the listed company's aggregated revenue despite the fact that foreign investors do not hold the legal title of the shares of the VIE.

The series of contracts generally include the following:[12]

(a) *Loan Agreement.* WFOEs incorporated in China are heavily regulated. Therefore, they can only work as a conduit to bring onshore foreign investment raised by ListCo. Instead of providing equity directly to OpCo, a WFOE lends the money to OpCo's Chinese shareholders on an interest free basis for the sole purpose of injecting capital into the OpCo. The loan agreement will generally contain a covenant to prohibit shareholders from misusing their position to transfer business, assets or intellectual property out of the OpCo.

(b) *Proxy Agreement.* In consideration of the loan advanced by the WFOE, the Chinese shareholders of the OpCo will give up their shareholders' rights, for example, attending and voting at shareholders' meetings. The Chinese shareholders will appoint the WFOE as their proxy to exercise these rights as WFOE sees fit. Together with the shareholders' personal rights, the entitlement to dividend is also passed onto the WFOE.

(c) *Technical Services Agreement.* In order for the WFOE to extract the retained profits within the OpCo, the WFOE will also enter into a technical services agreement with the OpCo, which is a sham contract that shifts retained profits in guise of a services fee paid to the WFOE.

---

10 Li Guo, 'Chinese Style VIEs: Continuing to Sneak Under Smog?' (2014) 47 (3) *Cornell International Law Journal* 570 at 577.

11 Jenny Li Zhang, 'Economic Consequences of Recognizing Off-Balance Sheet Activities', *AAA 2009 Financial Accounting and Reporting Section (FARS) Paper* (5 January 2009): SSRN: <http://dx.doi.org/10.2139/ssrn.1266456>.

12 Above n5 at 113–14.

(d) *Equity Pledge Agreement.* To secure all the contractual obligations of either the Chinese Shareholder or the OpCo, the WFOE will enter into an equity pledge agreement with the Chinese shareholders: the shares of the OpCo are pledged to secure the performance of the proxy agreement as well as directing the OpCo to comply with the Technical Services Agreement. However, the remedies under the equity pledge agreement are primarily intended to collect debts owed to the WFOE by the OpCo or their Chinese shareholders under the contractual arrangements. It does not give the WFOE any proprietary interest in the assets or shares of the OpCo.

(e) *Exclusive Call Option Agreement.* To make sure that the WFOE is able to recover the direct control of the assets or shares of the OpCo, should any of the Chinese shareholders go rogue, the WFOE will enter into an exclusive call option agreement to allow the WFOE to buy the OpCo's shares from the Chinese shareholders at a nominal value, and will take out another call option to buy OpCo's assets at the book value.

In summary, the Chinese shareholders of the OpCo are merely the *de jure* owners of VIE and whose names appear on the shareholders' register. The de facto owner is the WFOE and the ultimate beneficial owner will be the investors in ListCo that have gained the control and retain the benefits through various contracts.

The diagram below (Figure 1) explains how a textbook VIE structure works, in a nutshell.[13]

Figure 1

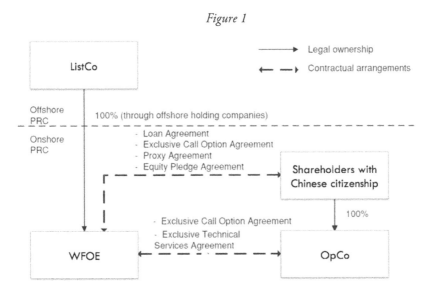

---

13 The diagram is adapted from a similar diagram contained in the Alibaba Group Annual Report 2017, n5 at 113.

The Alibaba's VIE structures are far more comprehensive and complex than the above example. As a comparison, the diagram below (Figure 2), was provided by the Alibaba Group in its financial report to illustrate its vast organisational structure.[14] Over half of Alibaba's 630 subsidiaries and other consolidated entities were established in a jurisdiction that is not China. Not surprisingly, most of the entities are in offshore financial centres, such as the Cayman Islands, the British Virgin Islands or Hong Kong.[15] Further, the registered office of the holding company in the Alibaba Group is located in the Cayman Islands at the offices of Trident Trust Company (Cayman) Limited, one of the largest offshore company service providers in the world.[16]

Despite seemingly working the magic of keeping up the appearance without sacrificing any control or benefit, there is certain price to pay to invest in a VIE structure.

Risks and challenges

When interviewed by CNBC, at its successful IPO, and asked to address the investors' concerns about interference of the government, transparency in its books and regulation, Jack Ma, the founder and executive chairman of Alibaba Group, mentioned that trust is the key.[17] This is essentially true as the shareholders of Alibaba Group have few legal options.

Jurisdiction issue

The series of contractual arrangements in a VIE structure generally provide that the contracts are governed by Chinese law and provide for the resolution of disputes through arbitration or court proceedings in China.

However, there are very few precedents and little guidance from the Chinese regulator as to how these VIE contracts should be interpreted or enforced in accordance with Chinese law.

Legal status recognition challenge

The lack of clarity concerning VIE contracts arises from the challenge in the Contract Law of the People's Republic of China. In particular, Article 52 of the Contract Law introduces at sub-section (3) the principle of substance over form that can nullify a

14 Above n5 at 111.

15 Ibid.

16 Memorandum of association of Alibaba Group Holding Limited (Amended and Re-stated by Special Resolution adopted on 15 September 2012 with effect from 18 September 2012).

17 Reuters and CNBC, 'Alibaba IPO biggest ever; shares decline': <https://www.cnbc.com/2014/09/22/alibaba-the-biggest-ever-ipo-after-more-shares-sold.html>.

Figure 2

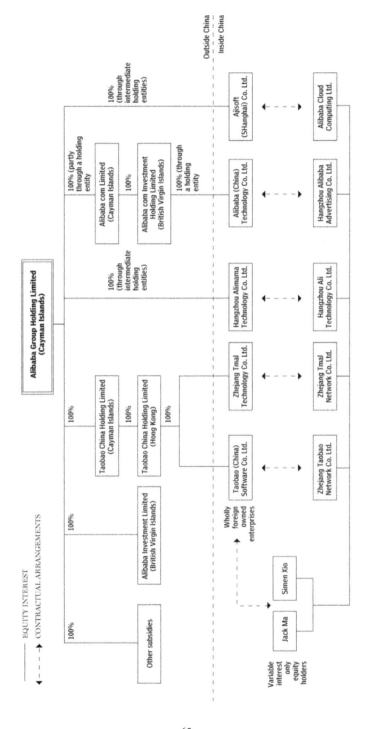

contract that intends to conceal an illegitimate purpose using a legal form, as well as at sub-section (5) the principle of illegality that can void a contract that violates the mandatory provisions of laws and administrative regulations.[18]

There is no clear definition of 'an illegitimate purpose' in subsection (3). It is open to contention that circumventing China's restrictions on foreign investment amounts to an illegitimate purpose. The 'laws' in subsection (5) refer to legislation implemented by the National People's Congress or its Standing Committee, and 'administrative regulations' refers to secondary legislation issued by the State Council, excluding rules circulated by ministries and commissions of the central government. Such fine nuances can determine the outcome of a case concerning the enforceability of VIE contracts in the Supreme People's Court.

Traditionally, the courts and arbitral tribunals have, in a handful of cases, held the ground that VIE structure is explicitly designed to circumvent the limitations on ownership and control by foreign investors, and thus VIE contracts are void at the outset.

The Shanghai Sub-Commission of the China International Economic and Trade Arbitration Commission determined the case of GigaMedia Limited, a Singaporean company listed on the Nasdaq in 2011. GigaMedia invested in T2CN Holding Limited, an online gaming business through a VIE structure. GigaMedia fell out with Wang Ji, the founder of T2CN, over issues relating to the control of the OpCo. While GigaMedia attempted to exercise its controlling power to replace Wang Ji as the CEO of the OpCo, Wang Ji applied for an arbitration award to declare all the VIE contracts void and severe the ties between GigaMedia's and the OpCo.[19] The Shanghai Sub-Commission found that the VIE structure violated the express prohibition of foreign investment in online gaming businesses in China. In accordance with Article 52 of the Contract Law, the VIE contracts were held to be invalid.[20]

The Supreme People's Court took a similar view in 2012 when determining whether Chinachem Financial Services Limited, a Hong Kong Company had invested in China Minsheng Banking Corporation by entering into an entrustment agreement in 1995, with China Small and Medium Enterprise Investment Development Limited (China SME), a Chinese company. The entrustment agreement was a less sophisticated arrangement than a standard suite of VIE contracts: China SME acted as a proxy to purchase and hold shares in Minsheng Bank on behalf of Chinachem. When a disagreement arose in relation to the dividend payments

---

18 《中华人民共和国合同法》 [Contract Law of the People's Republic of China], promulgated by the Second Sess. of the Ninth Nat'l People's Cong. (15 Mar. 1999).

19 Kenneth Kong and Shelly Sui, 'Shanghai CIETAC's Finding on VIE Case Raise Plenty of Questions' (2013) Jan *China Business Law Journal* 90 at 91.

20 刘燕[Liu Yan] 《在'默认合法'中爆发的法律风险－协议控制VIE模式下风险事件及案例述评》 [Legal Risks in the Presumption of Legality – Case Studies of the Contractual Arrangement of the VIE Structure] (2013) 9 《证券法苑》 [Securities Law Review] 1 at 22.

between Chinachem and China SME, the dispute led to a 12 year-long proceeding that ended up in the Supreme People's Court.[21] The Court found that the clear intention of the entrustment agreement was to circumvent the prohibition of foreign investment in the financial industry and thus had an illegitimate purpose, thereby making the entrustment agreement void.[22] On one hand, the simplicity in this one layer of contract perhaps to a certain extent made the court readier to pierce the contractual relationship. On the other hand, the most prevalent VIE structure these days will have a separate technology or consultancy services agreement to transfer the profits from the OpCo to WFOE in a more disguised fashion, making the court more reluctant to disrupt the VIE structure as a whole.

In 2014, the Supreme People's Court struck again, but in a completely different direction. In 2009, Changsha Yaxing Properties Development Co. Limited (Yaxing) entered into a framework agreement to transfer 70 per cent of the equity in two of their schools (Framework Agreement) to Beijing Normal University Ambow Education Technology Co. Ltd (Ambow), a Chinese company. In consideration of the 70 per cent equity, Ambow agreed to pay half of the price in cash and the other half with shares of Ambow Education Holding Ltd, a Cayman Island company (Ambow Holding). In 2010, Ambow entered into a series of VIE contracts, becoming the OpCo. Beijing Ambow Online Software Co. Ltd was the WFOE responsible for bringing in the funds raised by Ambow Holding from overseas. The share price of Ambow Holding tumbled quickly after its IPO, making the other half price paid to Yaxing worth next to nothing. Subsequently, Yaxing brought a case against Ambow to nullify the Framework Agreement. Yaxing's main claim [23] was that Ambow was merely a façade to conceal foreign investment in compulsory education, which is prohibited by the Catalogue for the Guidance of Foreign Investment Industries (Catalogue), promulgated by the Ministry of Commerce, and the National Development and Reform Commission. Thus it argued that the Framework Agreement was in breach of the Catalogue and should be held void.[24]

The Court, this time, decided to read down the authority of the Catalogue, which is an annexure to the Provision on Guiding the Orientation of Foreign Investment issued by the State Council (Provision). Prior to this decision, the

---

21 Paul Gillis and Michelle Lowry, 'Son of Enron: Investors Weigh the Risks of Chinese Variable Interest Entities' (2014) 26 *Journal of Applied Corporate Finance* 61at 64.

22 华懋金融服务公司诉中国中小企业投资服务公司[Chinachem Financial Services Limited v China Small and Medium Enterprise Investment Development Limited] (2002) 民四终字第30号[Civil Four Division Final Trial No. 30].

23 《指导外商投资方向规定》[Provisions on Guiding the Orientation of Foreign Investment] promulgated by State Council on 1 April 2002.

24 长沙亚兴置业发展有限公司诉北京师大安博教育科技有限责任公司 [Changsha Yaxing Properties Development Co. Ltd v Beijing Normal University Ambow Eduaction Technology Co. Ltd] (2014) 民一终字第24号 [Civil One Division Finial Trial No. 24].

common interpretation was that as part of the Provision, the Catalogue had the same effectiveness of administrative regulation as the Provision despite the fact that it is made by the government agency inferior to the State Council. In the case of *Yaxing v Ambow*, the Court applied the First Interpretation by the Supreme People's Court on Application of the Contract Law in that the Contract Law should be interpreted in accordance with laws made by NPC and its standing committee as well as administrative regulations made by the State Council, not laws or regulations made by local congress and government or rules made by ministries or departments.[25] In other words, the Court has avoided applying Article 52(5) of the Contract law to that the Framework Agreement and upheld the validity of the Framework Agreement albeit that it contradicted the Catalogue.[26]

The Supreme People's Court's judgment enhances the confidence of foreign investors in the VIE structure. However, it should be noted that the restrictions that are applicable to online platforms are regulated by the Provisions on the Administration of Foreign-funded Telecommunications Enterprises, which is a State Council regulation. In other words, if the validity of Alibaba Group's VIE contracts was challenged in the court today, it is doubtful if the court would follow the Supreme People's Court's decision in Ambow.

The rising threat on the horizon

There is also a threat of a new foreign investment laws on the horizon. On 19 January 2015, the Ministry of Commerce published the Foreign Investment Law Draft and Illustration for public submission (Draft). The proposed Draft introduces a principle of 'actual control', which is defined as having the power to exert decisive influence, via contractual or trust arrangements, over the subject entity's operations, financial, staffing and technology matters.[27] There have been commentaries which have suggested that this principle is designed to outlaw VIEs completely: under the proposed rule the foreign investors will be considered the actual controller of a VIE and thus the licence held in the OpCo's name will be invalidated.[28]

There is a saying – when the government closes a door, they also open a window. The Draft also provides that when a company is registered in a foreign jurisdiction but is actually controlled by a person of Chinese nationality (either a Chinese state-

---

25 《最高人民法院关于适用<合同法>若干问题的解释（一）》[the First Interoperation by the Supreme People's Court on Application of the Contract Law], Article 4.

26 Above n24.

27 《外国投资法（草案征求意见稿）》[Foreign Investment Law Draft] issued on 19 January 2015, Article 18 (3).

28 许浩[Xu Hao], '《外国投资法》草案征建议 互联网产业或被冲击'[The Internet Industry will take a blow in accordance with the Foreign Investment Law Draft],《中国经营报》*China Business Journal*, 25 January 2015: <http://tech.sina.com.cn/i/2015-01-25/doc-iavx-eafs0389230.shtml>.

owned enterprise, an agency or citizens), such company can submit supporting materials to have its investments determined by the relevant authority as Chinese investments.[29] This provision, once enacted, will inject more certainty in the VIE structure used by Alibaba Group by virtue of the existing Alibaba Partnership.

Alibaba Partnership

The Alibaba partnership is a mechanism designed to allow the business founder, as well as the management, to maintain control of the business they have built from scratch even when their founders' shares have been diluted by the IPO. It is only achievable in the securities markets that permit a listed company to issue two classes of shares. The most common dual-class share structure is that investors hold ordinary shares that carry one vote per share, while the founders or management hold weighted shares that carry multiple votes per share.[30]

Currently, only the stock markets in the United States, Brazil, Canada, France, Italy, Sweden, Switzerland, Denmark, Russia and Finland allow such shares.[31] The dual-class share structure disrupts the conventional idea that shareholders, by putting forward their capital and enduring the risks, should ultimately control the company. The notion of one share/one vote ensures, in a democratic way, that a shareholder has the amount of influence in the company that is equal to the amount of risk they take. Displacing this notion, the dual-share structure is likely to lead to management entrenchment.[32]

Despite such criticism, the enormous financial advantages, or perhaps the tremendous fear of missing out on another big whale like the Alibaba group, have lured more and more stock exchanges, such as London and Singapore, to float the possibility of opening up the market to dual-class shares companies.[33] In February 2017, in a discussion paper on the effectiveness of its markets, the UK regulator floated the possibility of loosening its restrictions. The Singapore Exchange has also published a general announcement clarifying that their existing secondary listing framework has the flexibility to accommodate dual-class shares companies.[34]

---

29 Above n27, article 45.

30 Joel Seligman, 'Equal Protection in Shareholder Voting Rights: The One Common Share, One Vote Controversy' (1986) 54 *The George Washington Law Review* 687 at 687.

31 Andrea Tan and Benjamin Robertson, 'Why Investors Are Fretting Over Dual-Class Shares', *Bloomberg Business Week* (10 July 2017): <https://www.bloomberg.com/news/articles/2017-07-10/why-investors-are-fretting-over-dual-class-shares-quicktake-q-a>.

32 Katie Bentel and Gabriel Walter, 'Dual Class Shares' (2016) *Comparative Corporate Governance and Financial Regulation*, Paper 2 at 18: <http://scholarship.law.upenn.edu/sch_2016/2>.

33 Above n31.

34 Singapore Exchange Limited, 'General Announcement: SGX clarifies that existing secondary listing framework allows dual class share companies' (28 July 2017): <http://infopub.

However, the Alibaba Partnership that has been allowed to list on the NYSE has an unorthodox dual-share structure in that it does not give the individual partners of the Alibaba Partnership weighted shares to concentrate control within the individual founders. Instead, the Alibaba Partnership as a whole has been conferred with the exclusive right to appoint up to a simple majority of the members of the board, defeating any majority shareholder's attempts to take over the company by taking control of the board.[35] The Alibaba Partnership structure has been promoted as a solution to preserving the corporate culture shaped by the founders while at the same time enhancing the collective responsibility.[36] However, the structure may also reflect the distrust of the founders who fear that individual members of the management may go rogue and hijack the company. Currently the Alibaba Partnership has 36 members including 27 members of management and nine members of management of Ant Financial Services and each of them has one vote in all partnership votes.[37] The number of partners in the Alibaba Partnership is not fixed and can be reduced by the retirement or departure of partners or increased by the election of new partners.[38] One matter that is reasonably clear is that most of partners are Chinese citizens.[39] Nevertheless, the unique structure poses the question who has the ultimate actual control of Alibaba Group – the Alibaba Partnership dominated by Chinese or the foreign investors?

Despite being a contractual arrangement, the Alibaba Partnership essentially gives the Chinese partners the power to direct the company by having control over the personnel on the board. When applying the definition of 'actual control' in the new draft Foreign Investment Law, an inference can be drawn that the VIE structure is ultimately controlled by Chinese citizens.

Conclusions – The Alternative Way Out

The Alibaba Partnership may resolve the concern over the legal risks and challenges of a VIE structure, but the question is still open as to how to make sure the best interests of the shareholders are properly represented in a complex group of companies.

Perhaps an alternative pathway to preserving the foreign investors' interests is to

---

sgx.com/Apps?A=COW_CorpAnnouncement_Content&B=AnnouncementToday&F=-794JA6LZ35VFIZTJ&H=061148532c22392567b832d509e3679bac44947309576cfdcb-fbf33d11d40007>.

35 Above n6 at 181.

36 Above n6 at 170.

37 Ibid. The Ant Financial Services is a related entity that controls Alipay, Alibaba's digital payment system which has been previously spun off by Jack Ma from the VIE structure through a series of public stunts which, to this day, are still haunting him.

38 Above n36.

39 Above n6 at 172–3.

increase scrutiny over the discharge of the directors' duties. It is doubtful that any foreign investors are more interested in running an e-commerce giant in a completely culturally different market on the other side of the globe than earning the dividends and increasing their wealth through the investment in Alibaba Group. Therefore, the main goal of the alternative pathway can be simplified as to prevent the management of Alibaba Group, the partners of the Alibaba Partnership, the shareholders and directors of OpCos from breaching the VIE contracts, shifting profits, businesses and assets from the VIE structure, and reducing the overall value of the ordinary shares held by foreign investors.

The overlapping of personnel between Alibaba Group, the Alibaba Partnership and their OpCos in China will make it possible to run a case against the same group of people for breaching fiduciary duties on the basis that their power over the OpCos are simply vested by virtue of being the directors and management of Alibaba Group. The other obvious advantage to choosing this cause of action is that the jurisdiction and governing law can be nominated in the company's constitution and the remedies available to the shareholders are not limited to damages. This proposal itself merits its own chapter and future research.

Chapter 7

Assessing the Risks of Money Laundering and Terrorist Financing through Companies and Trusts

Dr Gordon Hook

Introduction

In 1989 the Financial Action Task Force (FATF) was established by G-7 member states, the European Commission and a number of other OECD countries. It was formed in response to the threat posed to the international financial system by the laundering of illicit proceeds from drug trafficking and other serious crimes. Initially, its mandate was to examine money-laundering trends, review action at a national and international level, and develop measures to combat money laundering. Around this time other similar organisations were formed around the globe, called 'FATF-style regional bodies,' or FSRBs. It was hoped to bring the largest number of countries possible into a world-wide network of anti-money laundering bodies with a common purpose and policy direction. In 1997, the Asia/Pacific Group on Money Laundering (APG) was formed, which today is the largest FSRB in terms of geographic size and membership numbers, with 41 member jurisdictions and a large number of observer jurisdictions and organisations.

The FATF's establishment was preceded, in 1988, by the *United Nations Convention against Illicit Traffic in Narcotic Drugs and Psychotropic Substances.*[1] Article 3 of that convention imposed a requirement on countries to criminalise money laundering in relation to drug trafficking. In April 1990, the FATF issued a report containing a set of forty recommendations which expanded measures to combat money laundering beyond drug trafficking. In 1998 the United Nations issued a political declaration urging countries that had not yet done so to '… adopt by the year 2003 national money-laundering legislation and programmes.'[2] The

---

1 Article 3(1)(b)(i), (ii).

2 UN General Assembly (1998) A/RES/S-20/2. The time-line to 2003 proved more aspirational than achievable. In 2016 some counties still lacked basic laws, including criminal offences, to address money laundering. However, some FSRBs, including the Asia/Pacific Group on Money Laundering, used the five-year time line (1998–2003) as a bench mark to take membership-related action against members who joined (even after 2003) but following the expiry of five years had not implemented these obligations, which proved successful in pressuring those members to enact and implement relevant laws.

FATF's mandate expanded in 2001 beyond money laundering to include terrorist financing following the 11 September 2001 terror attacks and the issuance of United Nations Security Council Resolution 1373. The mandate was again expanded in 2012 to include a focus on proliferation financing in relation to weapons of mass destruction.

In each of the sets of FATF recommendations, companies, and later trusts, were singled out as vehicles which may be exploited to launder criminal funds. Accordingly, countries are required to adopt measures to address those concerns. Over the preceding twenty-seven years the importance of addressing the risks posed by those structures had grown.

Today, the FATF is the acknowledged international standard-setter for anti-money laundering and countering terrorist-financing measures with an ambitious programme of policy making; peer-reviewing member countries for their compliance with the standards; identification of money-laundering and terrorist-financing trends and techniques (typologies) and leadership among the global network of FSRBs. In 2005 the United Nations Security Council 'strongly urged' all member states to implement the international standards embodied in the FATF's forty recommendations.[3] In 2006 the United Nations General Assembly repeated the same encouragement.[4]

A major focus of the 2012 revised version of FATF forty recommendations is on identifying and understanding money-laundering and terrorist-financing risks and implementing domestic programmes to address and mitigate those risks using a risk-based approach. This chapter will look at the FATF requirements on assessing risks in relation to companies and trusts, and how well countries are doing in complying with those requirements. It will first look at the FATF requirements in general and then look at those requirements as they relate to companies and trusts.

Assessing Risk

In 2010 the FATF issued its first global assessment of money-laundering and terrorist-financing threats and identified various company structures and trusts as global 'enablers' of those threats.[5] The revised FATF recommendations of 2012 and the updated assessment methodology of 2013 focus largely on 'effectiveness' in implementation of the FATF standards and include a new standard requiring countries to understand their risks in order to use a risk-based approach to addressing

---

3 Other UNSCRs reference the FATF standards (e.g., 2083 and 2094). The International Monetary Fund and the World Bank accept reports from the FATF and FSRBs.

4 UN General Assembly (2006) Resolution 60/288.

5 FATF (2010), 'Global Money Laundering & Terrorist Financing Threat Assessment 2010', p.31. References in this chapter to FATF documents, including the FATF recommendations and assessment methodology, can be found at that FATF website: <www.fatf-gafi.org>.

the crimes of money laundering and terrorist financing. The FATF has also issued guidance to assist countries to develop those risk assessments.[6]

Recommendation 1 of the revised FATF forty recommendations provides, in part, that:

> Countries should identify, assess, and understand the money laundering and terrorist financing risks for the country, and should take action, including designating an authority or mechanism to coordinate actions to assess risks, and apply resources, aimed at ensuring the risks are mitigated effectively.[7]

It is important to note at the outset that the requirement here is that a country *identify, assess* and *understand* its risks and not that it produce a written or documented 'national risk assessment,' as is often assumed. The focus is on understanding not on documenting. However, having said that, and considering that the burden of proving that a country has identified, assessed and understands its risks is on the country under assessment and not on any third parties including assessors from the FATF or the Asia/Pacific Group on Money Laundering, it is difficult to imagine how a country can be said to *prove* that it understands its risks without having gone through a rigorous exercise culminating in the production of a written and comprehensive risk assessment. Conversely, a country that has produced a comprehensive national risk assessment document cannot be presumed to have met the burden of identifying, assessing and understanding its risk, as will be discussed below.

A second point to note about recommendation 1 is that the standard applies to a 'country' and not to the government (executive) alone. It goes beyond policy makers, regulators, supervisors and other relevant agencies and includes a consolidated or holistic national view involving the private sector. This does not, however, mean that the private sector is required to have the same views on risk as the government. Usually there are differences of opinion between government regulators and supervisors on some aspects of where the risks may be in specific delivery channels, products and clients amongst financial and non-financial institutions. For instance, if the government and banks are both in agreement that the banking sector is at high risk of money laundering given the nature of its products and services, but differ with respect to specific products, or specific services, this disagreement (all things considered) will not necessarily cast doubt on the credibility of the risk assessment and whether the country as a whole understands its risks. The FATF standards do not require a monolithic government-private sector view on all levels of risks. On the other hand, if there is a wholesale divergence of opinion between government and

---

6 FATF (2013) 'National Money Laundering and Terrorist Financing Risk Assessment Guidance 2013'.

7 FATF recommendation 1.

the banking sector on the levels of risk associated with the sector this may very well mean that the 'country' does not understand its risks, at least with respect to the banking sector. If the government is of the view that the banking sector as a whole is high risk, but the banking sector is of the view it is at low risk of money laundering and terrorist financing, there will be a problem. And that particular problem will be symptomatic of a broader problem, and not just with the manner in which an assessment was undertaken.

Another element of recommendation 1 is that countries should keep their risk assessments up to date. As circumstances change, risk assessments should be revised and updated accordingly. When the Panama paper revelations occurred in 2016, the nature of those revelations should have caused countries to revisit their risk assessments relevant to companies and trusts, update the analysis and address any issues identified.

An important aspect of FATF recommendation 1 which dovetails into the national risk assessment exercise is the following requirement on the private sector:

> Financial institutions and [designated non-financial businesses or professions] should be required to take appropriate steps to identify, assess, and understand their ML/TF risk [including] being required to: (a) document their risk assessments.[8]

Hence, while there is no technical requirement for a documented national-risk assessment adopted by a government, individual reporting entities such as banks, insurance companies, casinos, lawyers, accountants, etc. are required to document their risk assessments.

Throughout this chapter the term 'national risk assessment' will be used to refer to a money-laundering and terrorist-financing assessment undertaken at a national level (whether written or otherwise) in compliance with the requirements of FATF recommendation 1. We will also briefly look at the issues associated with the requirements on financial institutions and other reporting entities to undertake their own institutional risk assessments.

What is a National Risk Assessment?

A national money-laundering and terrorist-financing risk assessment is an organised and systematic effort by a country to identify and evaluate the sources and methods of money laundering and terrorist financing and to identify the weaknesses in that country's system.[9] The purpose of such an assessment is to assist national authorities to efficiently focus their resources giving priority to where the country's principal

---

8 The requirement to 'document' private-sector risk assessments is found in the Interpretive Note to recommendation 1.

9 FATF (2008), 'Money Laundering & Terrorist Financing Risk Assessment Strategies' at 5.

risks are. They can then inform financial and non-financial institutions of the assessment outcomes to assist them with their own internal risk assessments and to implement policies and procedures to address their own institutional risks through a risk-based approach.[10]

The FATF has developed a (somewhat artificial) analytical framework for understanding money-laundering and terrorist-financing risk. The framework involves three basic and inter-connected concepts, namely: threats, vulnerabilities and consequences.[11] Threats are defined as persons, objects or activities with potential to cause harm, for example, criminals or terrorists. Vulnerabilities are those things that can be 'exploited by the threat,' for example a lack of law or regulation or a particular product that is attractive to criminals. Finally, consequences are the impact of the threats that exploit vulnerabilities. While conceptually this framework is simple, it is artificial in the sense that when the FATF uses the term 'risk' in some of its literature it appears to use it inter-changeably with 'threats' or simply with the level of certain crime types in countries. However, the framework is a useful starting point for understanding risk. But it should not be employed in a risk-assessment exercise as a strict analytical framework. The concept of risk is a complex one and does not easily fit within the tight confines defined by the FATF.[12]

In assessing the risks of money laundering and terrorist financing through companies and trust arrangements, countries must understand, *within their own domestic context*, what types of corporate entities and legal arrangements are at risk of exploitation and *how* they are exploited given their country's unique risks and individual context. The FATF does not stipulate the manner in which a country should undertake an assessment. However, it is not enough for a country simply to survey global risks through typologies' reports published by the FATF or other similar bodies and incorporate that information into a national assessment. Because every country has factors and issues that make it unique, countries must be specific to their own domestic circumstances and context. While this may sound trite, it might be (and in some cases has been) tempting for countries to save time and energy assessing a sector it thinks is low risk (for instance, precious metal dealers) and incorporate public information from other countries or organisations supporting that conclusion without surveying their own sector and taking account of their own unique risks and context.

Moreover, a country may have undertaken a comprehensive risk-assessment

---

10 FATF (2013) 'National Money Laundering and Terrorist Financing Risk Assessments', FATF Guidance 2013.

11 Id at 7.

12 As one academic put it, the '… FATF has not yet been able to reach consensus about the definition of risk.' Louis De Koker, 'The 2012 Revised FATF Recommendations: Assessing and Mitigating Mobile Money Integrity Risks within The New Standards Framework' (2012) *Washington Journal of Law, Technology & Arts* 8,183.

exercise but, despite that, does not fully understand its risks. This may occur where a country engages an independent consultant to prepare, or facilitate in the preparation of, an assessment but not fully engage, or indeed engage at all, with the private sector, or in some cases with other relevant government agencies. It is difficult to imagine an effective and comprehensive risk assessment without all stakeholders engaged in the process, but in particular the private sector. Private-sector financial and non-financial institutions understand their customers, products and risks better than government agencies and ministries. Without the insight of private-sector institutions in the identification and evaluation phase of an assessment it would be difficult, if not impossible, for the government to appreciate and understand money-laundering and terrorist-financing risks in the various sectors it regulates. In the 2015 APG mutual evaluation report of Vanuatu, it was noted that while there was a comprehensive and written national risk assessment of money laundering and terrorist financing across all sectors and various crime types, many government agencies and most private-sector reporting entities '… seemed to be unaware of its existence or the process leading to its completion. Even those agencies that were aware of the existence of the draft document were unfamiliar with its actual content and its policy and operational implications.'[13] It is not surprising that one of the conclusions reached in that report was that Vanuatu failed to understand its risks.

Before discussing private-sector risk assessment, there is one other point that can impact on whether a country can be said to understand its risks. Although FATF recommendation 1 talks about countries identifying 'higher risks' and 'lower risks'[14] it does not require that a risk rating be assigned to any particular risk identified and evaluated; however, it is not uncommon for countries to do that. A risk rating usually takes the form of assigning 'high risk', 'medium risk', or 'low risk' to an outcome. It may even assign ratings such as 'low–medium,' 'medium–high' and 'high–very high.' For instance, a country might indicate that the risk of money laundering associated with publicly traded companies is low, whereas the risk associated with shell companies is high. Likewise, with respect to trusts, an assessment might conclude that domestic trusts pose 'low' risk but foreign trusts governed by the laws of a specific tax haven are 'high' risk. If a country uses such a rating system it should have a definition for these terms and a methodology to assist in selecting them in any given circumstance. If authorities cannot explain what they mean in assigning such ratings it could be argued that they do not understand their risks. Could a country

13 APG (2015), *Anti-money laundering and counter-terrorist financing measures-Vanuatu*, Third Round Mutual Evaluation Report, APG (Sydney): <https://www.apgml.org/mutu-al-evaluations/documents/default.aspx?pcPage=2>.

14 Recommendation 1: 'Where countries identify higher risks, they should ensure that their [anti-money laundering and countering terrorist financing] regime adequately addresses such risks. Where countries identify lower risks, they may decide to allow simplified mea-sures for some of the FATF Recommendations under certain conditions.'

be said to understand the risk of money laundering via shell companies if it cannot explain why it assigned a rating of medium and not high? – arguably not. The point here is that a major purpose of a national-risk assessment is to respond to identified risks on a priority basis using a risk-based approach focusing more resources on high-risk money laundering and terrorist financing and fewer on lower risk areas. Using the 'high' to 'low' rating system will therefore have a major impact on resource allocation and risk mitigation.

Private-Sector Risk Assessments

As noted earlier, FATF recommendation 1 also requires that financial institutions and designated non-financial businesses and professions, such as lawyers, accountants, and trust and company-service providers, also undertake their own risk assessments and take effective action to mitigate their identified risks.

Like national-risk assessments, the FATF standards do not stipulate how private-sector reporting entities should conduct their own internal assessments. However the FATF recommendations do contain some additional requirements not applicable for national assessments.

> Private-sector entities must:
> - document their risk assessments;
> - consider all the relevant risk factors before determining what is the level of overall risk and the appropriate level and type of mitigation to be applied;
> - keep these assessments up to date; and
> - have appropriate mechanisms to provide risk-assessment information to competent authorities and [self-regulating bodies].[15]

Private-sector assessments take a different approach from national assessments. As noted by the Wolfsberg Group, 'most [financial institutions] will be used to assessing risk in areas such as credit risk or market risk, where risk can be easily quantified and is usually assessed prior to accepting that risk. A Financial Crime Risk Assessment, however, differs somewhat, focusing on assessing 'consequential' risk, i.e. risk that is reflective of a [financial institution's] internal and external environment, including mitigating controls.'[16] In addition, the size and scope of an institutional assessment will necessarily be different from the national assessment. As stated by the FATF in relation to banks:[17]

---

15 FATF Assessment Methodology, criterion 1.10.

16 Wolfsberg (2015), 'The Wolfsberg Frequently Asked Questions on Risk Assessments for Money Laundering, Sanctions and Bribery & Corruption': <https://www.wolfsberg-principles.com/pdf/faq/Wolfsberg-Risk-Assessment-FAQs-2015.pdf>.

17 FATF (2014), *Guidance for a Risk Based Approach, the Banking Sector*: <https://www.fatf-gafi.org/media/fatf/documents/reports/Risk-Based-Approach-Banking-Sector.pdf>.

A bank's risk assessment need not be complex, but should be commensurate with the nature and size of the bank's business. For smaller or less complex banks, (for example where the bank's customers fall into similar categories and/or where the range of products and services the bank offers are very limited), a simple risk assessment might suffice. Conversely, where the bank's products and services are more complex, where there are multiple subsidiaries or branches offering a wide variety of products, and/or their customer base is more diverse, a more sophisticated risk assessment process will be required.

Assessing risk goes beyond the mere collection of quantitative and qualitative information. Private-sector entities should be aware of the difference between 'inherent risk' associated with the nature of delivery channels of products and customers, on the one hand and 'residual risk' which is the remaining risk posed to the institution as a result of applying mitigating measures. Information in relation to both should be kept up to date and informative enough to allow any given institution to adapt to changing circumstances. Moreover, internal institutional assessments will be informative information for governments undertaking the process leading to national risk assessments.

Assessing the Risk posed by Companies and Trusts

Companies[18]

In addition to the general requirements of recommendation 1 outlined earlier, recommendation 24 specifically provides that 'countries should assess the ML/TF risks associated with all types of legal persons created in the country.'[19] The requirement associated with 'all types' of legal persons includes an analysis of domestic and foreign-registered companies, limited-liability partnerships, and other entities with legal personality. Although foreign companies are not 'created in the country' they must be registered in the country. The FATF has treated the foreign-company registration requirement as the same as establishment in the country.[20] With that in mind, a comprehensive risk assessment should include an assessment of the money-laundering and terrorist-financing risks associated with:

- public companies (whether listed or not);
- private and closely held companies;
- companies formed in foreign jurisdictions but registered in the country assessing its own risks;

18 For the purposes of this article the terms 'companies' and 'corporations' will be treated as referring to the same type of entity and the term 'company' will be used to refer to both.

19 FATF (2013), Assessment Methodology, recommendation 24.2.

20 See for example the joint FATF/APG mutual evaluation of Singapore at: FATF and APG (2016), *Anti-money laundering and counter-terrorist financing measures-Singapore,* Fourth Round Mutual Evaluation Report, FATF, Paris and APG, Sydney: <https://www.fatf-gafi. org/publications/mutualevaluations/documents/mer-singapore-2016.html>.

- companies without share capital; and
- companies limited by guarantee.[21]

Each type of company poses its own unique risk. And within each category there may be specific forms that merit attention. For example, a number of countries have identified particular forms of private companies as posing a substantial risk for money laundering:

> Front companies, shell companies and shelf companies are misused for illicit purposes, often (in the case of front companies) by intermingling of licit and illicit profits. The US has reported that shell companies (primarily in the form of corporations and LLCs) pose the biggest risk, although the risk is mitigated by some factors including the ability of [law enforcement authorities] to investigate relevant bank records, tax filings and other documents to obtain information about beneficial owners, living and/or having operations in the US.[22]

Special and unique forms of private companies such as 'protected cell companies' or 'look-through companies' (the latter is a New Zealand form of company with special tax benefits) may also pose unique risks and should be examined as part of the assessment process.

For the most part, it is true to say that publicly traded companies have less risk of money laundering and terrorist financing than closely held private companies. Publicly traded companies have more robust disclosure requirements and are subject to regulation and supervision by agencies such as securities commissions. Private companies do not have such measures in place (for the most part). But, as noted above, a country cannot assume this to be the case and must consider the risk posed by any companies within its own domestic context.

Whatever the risk posed by corporate entities, the process used to assess the risks should include an initial inventory of the forms of legal persons available or operating in the country, consultation across relevant government agencies including company registries, tax authorities, law-enforcement agencies, securities commissions, etc. as well as consultation with the private sector including lawyers, accountants, professional company secretaries and other relevant entities that may form or manage such entities.

---

21 Other types of legal persons such as associations, incorporated societies should be assessed as well.

22 FATF (2016), *Anti-money laundering and counter-terrorist financing measures-United States,* 4th Mutual Evaluation Report, FATF, Paris, at 223: <https://www.fatf-gafi.org/publications/mutualevaluations/documents/mer-united-states-2016.html>. See the following chapter which deals with 'shell' and 'shelf' companies.

Trusts

While recommendation 25 makes specific reference to 'express trusts' (defined in the glossary to the recommendations as not including constructive, resulting or other forms of implied trusts) the recommendation goes beyond that to include other types of legal arrangements that are similar to trusts. A footnote to recommendation 25 in the 2013 assessment methodology states that:

> The measures required by recommendation 25 are set out with specific reference to trusts. This should be understood as referring to express trusts (as defined in the glossary). In relation to other types of legal arrangements with a similar structure or function, countries should take similar measures to those required for trusts, with a view to achieving similar levels of transparency ...

Unlike an assessment of legal persons, the FATF recommendations relevant to trusts do not contain a separate requirement to assess all types of trusts. It is not clear from the text why this is so. However, a risk assessment should nonetheless include an assessment of all types as part of the general risk-assessment requirements of recommendation 1. The types of express trusts that should be assessed include fixed trusts, discretionary trusts, foreign trusts, and unique forms of business trusts if they exist in the jurisdiction. One unique form of trust is a so-called 'flee trust' (discussed in the next chapter) which poses unique risks.

One of the major vulnerabilities associated with trusts is their lack, in most countries, of oversight through a registry or regulation mechanism. Unlike companies, trusts are not generally required to be registered in order to have legal effect nor are there, for the most part, any government entities which maintain supervisory oversight for their operations.[23] Although trusts with tax implications mean that the trustees of those trusts are required to file tax returns, not all trusts file tax returns. Moreover, the filing of trust tax returns cannot be considered a form of registration or regulation in the sense of amounting to mitigation measures for money laundering and terrorist financing especially in light of the fact that in many jurisdictions tax secrecy laws will protect the sharing of any information filed with taxation authorities, including with law enforcement authorities.

As with companies, when a country undertakes a money-laundering and terrorist-financing risk assessment of trusts it should first make a list of relevant trusts that operate in the country and then establish a consultation mechanism including relevant-government agencies and private-sector entities including those involved in forming or managing trusts.

---

23 There are some exceptions. For instance, in South Africa, all *inter-vivos* trusts involving property that is located in South Africa must be registered under the *Trust Property Control Act* 1988 with a Master of the High Court, regardless of where the settler, trustee or beneficiaries are located. Trusts are usually registered in the jurisdiction where the trust assets are located.

Assessing Risk Associated with Designated non-Financial Businesses and Professions (DNFBPS)

A major component of assessing risks associated with companies and trusts is assessing risks related to designated non-financial businesses and professions or simply 'DNFBPs' which can facilitate the establishment and maintenance of those structures. DNFBPs are defined in the FATF assessment methodology as including casinos, real-estate agents, dealers in precious metals and precious stones, lawyers, notaries, other independent legal professionals and accountants and trust company service providers.[24] For our purposes, the relevant DNFBPs are lawyers, accountants and 'trust and company service providers' (TCSPs).

Lawyers and accountants

The formation and use of the various forms of companies and trusts can involve complex legal issues including tax implications. Lawyers and accountants are often consulted to provide advice and other services including contract drafting, drafting of trust deeds, acting as intermediaries with financial institutions and other services including use of trust or client accounts to transact business. FATF recommendation 22 requires lawyers and accountants to put in place certain preventive measures to mitigate the risk of money laundering and terrorist financing '... when they prepare for, or carry out, transactions for their client concerning the organisation of contributions for the creation, operation or management of companies; creating, operating or management of legal persons or arrangements; and buying and selling of business entities.[25] A risk assessment needs to take into account these services.

However, the legal and accounting professions may have different risks. In setting out to assess the levels of risk with lawyers and accountants, it is important to understand the two professions, what sets them apart, how large the two professions are, their makeup (firms, sole practitioners etc.) and the services they offer. One issue that sets lawyers apart from accountants is the concept of legal professional privilege. This may be viewed as a particular vulnerability for exploitation by criminals and may have a direct impact on risk levels for lawyers. Criminals may deliberately choose lawyers to provide incorporation or trust services in order to hide behind the veil created by this privilege.

Consultation with both professions is paramount and should include reference to internal risk assessments undertaken by both professions to understand how they see their own risk with respect to different clients, services and undertakings.

---

24 FATF Assessment Methodology, Glossary.

25 FATF Assessment Methodology criterion 22.1(d).

Trust and company service providers (TCSPs)

A TCSP is defined within the wider definition of DNFBPs to mean a person or business that:[26]

- acts as a formation agent of legal persons;
- acts as (or arranges for another person to act as) a director or secretary of a company, a partner of a partnership, or a similar position in relation to other legal persons;
- provides a registered office; business address or accommodation, correspondence or administrative address for a company, a partnership or any other legal person or arrangement;
- acts as (or arranges for another person to act as) a trustee of an express trust or performing the equivalent function for another form of legal arrangement; or
- acts as (or arranging for another person to act as) a nominee shareholder for another person.

Of course many of these functions may also be exercised by a lawyer or an accountant. A formation agent (first bullet point) is designed to capture anyone who, in a business capacity as opposed to a 'one-off' undertaking, acts on behalf of someone else to form a company regardless of whether they have the authority to enter in legal contracts on behalf of the principal. More often than not TCSPs are incorporated entities offering a wide range of financial services in addition to the services listed by the FATF.

According to the Group of International Finance Centre Supervisors, TCSPs 'can fulfil an important role in ensuring that their organisations are not used as a conduit for financial crime such as money laundering, bribery and corruption and tax evasion, or the holding of stolen assets.'[27] However, the World Economic Forum, has expressed concern that TCSPs may be involved either knowingly or unknowingly in money laundering and financing of terrorism schemes:

> Given their trusted gatekeeper status, professionals can misuse the absence of direct supervision to launder funds themselves and/or act as 'good faith' intermediaries in helping others to launder. This can occur in a variety of contexts, such as the securities and derivatives markets, the real estate market, etc., only some of which are discussed here. Active criminal infiltration of professional roles or subornation of existing professionals are key routes to criminal success.[28]

---

26 FATF Assessment Methodology, Glossary.

27 Group of International Finance Centre Supervisors (2014), 'Standard on the Regulation of Trust and Corporate Service Providers', at 5: <https://www.gifcs.org/images/GIFCSStandardonTCSPs.pdf>.

28 World Economic Forum (2012), 'Organized Crime Enablers', July 2012, at 34: <https://www.reports.weforum.org/organized-crime-enablers-2012/#chapter-enablers-of-money-laundering>.

When assessing the risk of money laundering and terrorist financing associated with TCSPs the same scoping exercise used for lawyers and accountants should be undertaken. An inventory of TCSPs operating in the country should be created together with a breakdown of the nature of the TCSP business (incorporated business, partnership etc.) and consultation across all relevant government agencies and private-sector entities.

Challenging a National Risk Assessment

One final point before looking at the compliance levels across the countries that have already been assessed under the FATF's 2012 recommendations.

When the FATF and other assessing bodies assess a country for compliance with the FATF standards, the assessors are not bound to accept the results of a national risk assessment. Those standards require assessors to examine critically the assessment presented to them. 'There may be cases where assessors cannot conclude that the country's assessment is reasonable, or where the country's assessment is insufficient or non-existent.'[29] This does not mean that assessors are required to undertake their own risk assessment of the country under examination but they may use open-source material, media reports and other information to question the methodology of the risk assessment and its results.

For example, if a country under assessment produces a national risk-assessment document which indicates that the risk of money laundering in the country through trusts is low, but the jurisdiction under assessment is an off-shore tax haven with trust secrecy laws, assessors would be justified in being sceptical. Those assessors could consult external publications, including World Bank and International Monetary Fund reports, media reports and academic publications, to gain a deeper understanding of the environment. They can then use that understanding to question officials when in the country discussing the national assessment with officials and the private sector. It may be that the country is justified in its conclusions but the duty is on the assessors to question the reasonableness of the risk assessment.

Compliance Levels

Out of thirty-eight countries so far assessed under the FATF standards of 2012 to October 2017,[30] only twelve countries have received satisfactory ratings for recommendation 1.[31] With respect to recommendation 22 (DNFBPs), only fourteen countries were rated as satisfactory.

These rating are not fully reflective of the risks associated with companies and

---

29 FATF Assessment Methodology, paragraph 15.

30 See following chapter for a list of the countries assessed.

31 Satisfactory ratings are 'largely compliant' or 'compliant'. Unsatisfactory ratings are 'non-compliant' or partially compliant'.

trusts but they do indicate that compliance levels overall are not satisfactory when it comes to assessing and understanding money-laundering and terrorist-financing risk relating to companies and trusts. Effectively two-thirds of the countries already assessed are failing to implement satisfactory measures in relation to assessing and understanding risks as well as implementing mitigation measures to address risks. As more countries are assessed this ratio is likely to remain the same.

Conclusion

Assessing money-laundering and terrorist-financing risks, associated companies and trusts, as well as professionals who facilitate their formation and management, is a complex task involving a survey of the various structures that can be established in a country and an understanding of the unique context within which those structures operate. The international standards are clear: countries must identify, assess and understand their risks in their own unique contexts and put in place measures to mitigate those risks. However, so far, with thirty-eight countries already assessed against those standards, the majority are not measuring up to satisfactory marks in this area.

In the next chapter, we will see just how companies and trusts may be used to launder illicit funds or finance terrorists through company and trust structures.

Chapter 8

Beneficial Ownership and Control of Corporate and Trust Structures: Global AML/CFT Standards

Dr Gordon Hook

In April 2016, the G-20's finance ministers called on countries 'to improve the implementation of the international standards on transparency, including on the availability of beneficial ownership information of legal persons and legal arrangements, and its international exchange.'[1] Shortly afterwards, the Financial Action Task Force – as the international standard setter for beneficial ownership disclosure rules for companies and trusts – stated that 'the Panama papers were a timely reminder of the scale of abuse of companies and trusts for a range of illicit purposes. Improving transparency has become a global priority, and FATF will make proposals for improving implementation of the FATF standards.'[2]

This chapter will focus on how companies and trusts present inherent risks of exploitation for illicit purposes. It will also canvass what is required by the FATF standards for countries to address those risks and it will review the compliance levels by countries already assessed against the revised FATF standards of 2012.

Vulnerability of Companies and Trusts to Money Laundering

Given the ease with which a company or a trust can be established and the relatively low cost of doing so, as well as the nature and mechanisms available within company and trust structures, the vulnerabilities of those structures to money laundering is widely recognised.[3] In 2001 the OECD published the report, *Behind the Corporate Veil: Using Corporate Entities for Illicit Purposes* in which it acknowledged the important and legitimate roles of companies and trusts in the global economic system, but highlighted the potential of their misuse for money laundering, bribery, improper insider dealings, illicit tax practices, and other forms of criminal behaviour. '… [A]lmost every criminal act, including economic crimes, involves the use of legal

---

1 G20 Finance Ministers and Central Bank Governors' Communique (2016), paragraph 12: <http://www.g20.utoronto.ca/2016/ 160724-finance.html>.

2 FATF (18–24 June 2016), 'Summary of Outcomes of Financial Action Task Force Plenary week': <http://www.fatf-gafi.org/countries/j-m/korea/documents/fatf-plenary-week-june-2016.html>.

3 FATF and APG typologies reports are available from their websites.

persons, and … corporations throughout the world are used to launder money.'[4] The OECD noted that the principal forms of secrecy have shifted from individual bank accounts to corporate and trust bank accounts.

The concern has not been abated with the passage of time. More recent studies[5] and earlier statements by the G-20[6] have demonstrated that the use of companies and trusts in money laundering schemes is still prevalent despite changes to the FATF standards to address many of those concerns (discussed later in this chapter) and despite firm obligations on countries to implement those standards.

Below is a brief discussion of what mechanisms have been used by persons to exploit company and trust structures to launder criminal proceeds.

Shell companies

There is no legal definition of a 'shell company' but generally speaking shell companies are incorporated entities, usually with minimal paid-in capital, whose business objectives may be unknown, unclear or perhaps dubious, many or most of which lack employees and have few or no assets. They may and usually do, if incorporated in another jurisdiction, lack a physical presence in the jurisdiction in which they hold bank accounts unless the law under which they are incorporated requires a resident director. In that case, shell companies may employ an agent or nominee to act in that capacity.

While shell companies are often used for legitimate purposes, such as holding companies for corporate mergers or as management companies for businesses or rental properties, shell companies have been used to disguise the true ownership and source of illicit funds and to facilitate criminal fund transfers.[7] In a United Kingdom report dated 2000,[8] it was noted that 'almost all the most complex laundering operations involve UK shell companies.' A money launderer can form a shell company in one country owned by another shell company incorporated in a different country, use it to open a bank account, deposit illicit funds in that account then wire those funds overseas. Following that simple transaction, the company can be discarded by simply not paying annual filing fees to a company register. After a fixed period of time the company will automatically be dissolved for failure to pay the fee. The United States' Financial Crimes Enforcement Network

---

4 At <http://www.oecd.org/corporate/ca/43703185.pdf> at 13.

5 World Bank/UNODC (2011), 'The Puppet Masters', Stolen Asset Recovery Initiative 2011.

6 G20 (2014) 'High-Level Principles on Beneficial Ownership Transparency': <www.ag.gov.au/CrimeAndCorruption/AntiCorruption/Documents>.

7 See APG Typologies Report 2002; FATF Typologies Report 2002/2003.

8 UK Cabinet Office (2000), 'Recovery the Proceeds of Crime', at 85: <https://www.cabinetoffice.gov.uk/media/cabinetoffice/strategy/assets/crime.pdf>.

reported in 2006 that '… suspected shell companies incorporated or organized in the United States have moved billions of dollars globally from accounts at banks in foreign countries …'[9]

Shell companies have been used to hide the identities of politically exposed persons and other high-risk customers who would otherwise catch the attention of financial institutions for enhanced customer due diligence checks. For instance, in 2012 the High Court in London ordered that a property worth £10m owned in the name of 'Capitana Seas Limited,' a shell company registered in the British Virgin Islands and owned by the son of the former president of Libya, was an asset of the government of Libya. The court ordered the property to be returned to the Libyan government.[10]

Shell companies have also been used in 'sanctions busting' cases. A relatively recent case involved a shell company incorporated in New Zealand which had no assets, employees or physical presence anywhere. It leased a former Russian military cargo aircraft to carry weapons from DPRK (North Korea) through Bangkok, Thailand on its way to third party state:[11] all in breach of UN sanctions against DPRK. Its beneficial owners and those in control were difficult to identify (but eventually were).

The recent joint FATF and APG mutual evaluation report of Singapore observed that Singapore's national risk assessment on money laundering and terrorist financing identifies an increase in the number of money-laundering cases involving shell companies established by non-residents based overseas.[12]

Shelf companies

Shelf companies are simply companies that have been incorporated then left inactive until sold, sometimes for a number of years. Lawyers or other company-formation professionals may incorporate a number of companies, hold them in their office (or on their 'shelf'), maintain the corporate record filing requirements, then on-sell them to new clients seeking company incorporation.

Some of the legitimate reasons to purchase a shelf company include avoiding the delays that may occur while waiting for corporate registries to conclude the company registration process or to purchase a company that has an apparent life in order to

---

9 FINCEN (2006), 'The Role of Domestic Shell Companies in Financial Crime and Money Laundering': <https://www.fincen.gov/sites/default/files/shared/LLCAssessment_FINAL.pdf>.

10 *State of Libya v Capitana Seas Ltd.* [2012] EWHC 602 (Com).

11 *Sydney Morning Herald* (15 May 2011): <https://www.smh.com.au/national/inside-the-shell-drugs-arms-and-tax-scams-20110514-1enkz.html>.

12 FATF and APG (2016), *Anti-money laundering and counter-terrorist financing measures-Singapore,* Fourth Round Mutual Evaluation Report at 16, paragraph 40.

open an account with a financial institution which may require proof that a company has existed for a period of time before entering into the customer relationship.

The attraction for criminals is that shelf companies can be purchased and used in a very short time frame for the movement of illicit funds and then, if necessary, discarded in the same way as shell companies noted above.

Nominee shareholders

Nominee shareholders, sometimes referred to as trustee shareholders, hold company shares in their name on behalf of another person, whether a natural person or legal person. The actual beneficial owner of the shares is not listed in the company shareholder register – only the nominee is – thus according a degree of anonymity to the former. Usually the relationship between the nominee and the beneficial owner is reflected in a written instrument such as a trust deed, but written instruments are not necessarily required. Jurisdictions which permit nominee shareholders, but have no additional disclosure requirements in relation to the real owner, have heightened money-laundering risks.

Criminals can use third parties such as company-service providers, lawyers, accountants, friends and family members to hide their ownership from public disclosure. As one official stated: 'A non-transparent corporate structure is a breeding ground for money laundering, tax evasion, corruption and terrorist financing. Opponents of a secret beneficial ownership system also argue that it obstructs the free market because there is no true access to corporate information.'[13]

Many corporate and trust service providers, including some in Australia, openly advertise their firms as offering nominee shareholder services[14] with client secrecy. The FATF recommendations (discussed later in this chapter) extend to professionals that offer professional company secretaries or company-service providers.[15]

Nominee directors

Directors of companies may nominate proxies to act on their behalf or under their direction. Once formalised, the director's name is changed on the company records to the named proxy, sometimes referred to as a 'nominee director' or 'third party directors.' In Australia they are referred to as 'alternate directors.'[16] Alternatively,

---

13 Christine Duhaime (2013), 'Tax evasion, beneficial ownership and money laundering – what are the issues facing Canada at the G8 Summit next week?' (15 June 2013): <http://www.antimoneylaunderinglaw.com/2013/06/tax-evasion-beneficial-ownership-and-money-laundering-whats-the-connection-in-canada.html>.

14 A google search of the phrase 'nominee shareholder services' will reveal a plethora of firms which advertise this service.

15 FATF recommendation 22.

16 *Corporations Act* s. 201k.

on company incorporation a nominee may be the first to be registered as director through a formal nomination instrument from the 'real' or 'actual' director. In the latter case, the real director's name is absent from the company records from the beginning.

Many corporate service providers (including lawyers and accountants) offer nominee director services for their clients and many of the uses of these services are legitimate. For example, a director may nominate his or her lawyer or other nominee to act in their place while the director is overseas, incapacitated or otherwise absent or unable to perform the duties of director. On the other hand, the non-disclosure of the 'real' director affords a high degree of anonymity and therefore can be exploited for criminal purposes or gain where the owner and director of a shell company, for instance, wishes to hide his or her name from public view. In order to make the nominee director system work for criminal purposes, the nominee is appointed by the 'real director,' usually under an instrument of appointment (a declaration), and then signs back a power of attorney authorising the 'real director' to engage in the business as the director – i.e. investing criminal proceeds in the business in order to launder their appearance as legitimate. The nominee's name is merely a paper entry in the corporate registry office and in the corporate records but serves the purpose of masking the real director from public view.

Corporate directors

The business of a company is managed by or under the direction of directors and in doing so directors must exercise their powers and discharge their duties in good faith.[17]

Many jurisdictions permit incorporated companies to act as directors of other companies. Complex structures involving multiple companies in ownership tiers may use corporate directors legitimately. For instance, parent companies may wish to act as directors in their subsidiary entities. In other circumstances, professional company-service providers may be incorporated and so the use of their service involves corporate entities as directors.

However, the engagement of corporate directors is one more way a criminal may shield their identity from disclosure to authorities. A criminal could use an off-shore company he or she has incorporated in a 'secrecy jurisdiction' to act as director and shareholder in a shell company formed solely to launder funds. The added company layer (a company holding a directorship of another company) obscures ownership and control of the second shell from law enforcement and tax authorities in the event of a criminal investigation into money-laundering activity.

---

17 *Corporations Act* 2001, ss. 181 and 198A.

Bearer shares and bearer-share warrants

Shares represent a unit of ownership in a company. Generally speaking, there are different types of shares in a company. Common (or ordinary) shares usually have voting rights while preferred (or preference) shares, whose dividend payouts are made in priority to common shares, do not or may not have voting rights, but still represent a unit of ownership in the company.[18] Usually common and preferred shares have to be in registrable form, i.e. the owner of the share certificate is named in the company's shareholder register as the owner of that share.

Bearer shares are similar to other shares but there is no registered owner of such shares. Ownership is determined, or presumed, based on possession of a bearer-share certificate in the same way that ownership in a currency note is determined, or presumed, on the basis of possession of the note. Transfers of ownership occur by simple transfer of possession.[19] Ownership of a property right in a company can therefore be hidden from view with bearer-share certificates. Australia does not permit the issuance of bearer shares for companies incorporated under the *Corporations Act 2001*.[20]

A share warrant is not a share and does not represent a unit of ownership in a company. It is a document issued by a company 'certifying that the bearer is entitled to the shares specified in it.'[21] The name of the bearer does not appear on the register of members until he surrenders the warrant to the company in return for transfer of the shares, but he may be regarded as a company member under the provisions of the articles of association. The company is contractually bound to recognise the bearer as shareholder. Like bearer shares, bearer-share warrants are easily transferable. Transfer or delivery of the warrant operates as a transfer of the right to redeem the instrument for shares in the company. Australia does not prohibit the issuance of bearer-share warrants.

Both bearer shares and bearer-share warrants (including similar instruments issued by foreign companies registered in a jurisdiction which prohibits its

---

18 In Australia these shares are referred to as 'ordinary' and 'preference' shares (*Corporations Act* 2001, sections, 1.5.6 and 254a).

19 See definition of 'bearer share' in Glossary to Assessment Methodology 2013.

20 *Corporations Act* 2001, s. 254F.

21 The FATF methodology does not define what a share warrant is. However, the following is a definition:
'A [bearer] share warrant is a document issued by a company certifying that the bearer is entitled to the shares specified in it. The name of the bearer will not appear on the register of members until he surrenders the warrant to the company in return for transfer of the shares, but he may be regarded as a company member under the provisions of the articles of association. The company is contractually bound to recognize the bearer as shareholder.'
See, Oxford (2016), *Dictionary of Finance and Banking*: <https://www.oxfordreference.com/search?q=share+warrant &searchBtn = Search&isQuickSearch=true.>.

domestically formed companies from issuing them)[22] may be used in money-laundering schemes as they offer high degrees of ownership anonymity. And when coupled with other mechanisms mentioned above such as nominee directors and shareholders even further obfuscation of ownership can be achieved. A case in point to illustrate the degree of anonymity that may be achieved through the use of bearer-share warrants and nominee directors is the case of *Andre' Pascal Enterprises (England and Wales)*. The summary is cited in full in the World Bank's report of this case.[23]

André Pascal Enterprises was an England and Wales private company limited by shares (with bearer-share warrants) set up by a UK corporate service provider. Upon payment and submission of the order to set up the company, the provider electronically lodged the application with UK Companies House. The provider became the initial shareholder of the company and subscriber to the Memorandum and Articles of Association for the purposes of government records. Upon receipt of signed documents from the client – but without requiring or requesting the client to provide any supporting identification – the provider issued bearer-share warrants, erasing the provider's name from the share registry without substituting any other. André Pascal Enterprises had a nominee director and nominee secretary (courtesy of the provider), again providing separation from the beneficial owner. The incorporation process took less than a day, filling out the online forms took 45 minutes, and the total cost was £515.95.

Trusts

Trusts are not legal entities but describe a relationship between specific persons.[24] They may be created in most, if not all, common law countries and similar, but legally different, arrangements can be created in some civil law countries,[25] while

22 Singapore prohibits the issuance of bearer shares and bearer-share warrants for companies formed in Singapore, but it was noted in their recent mutual evaluation report that '… there are no mitigating measures in the *Companies Act* or elsewhere to address the risk posed by the same instruments that may be issued by foreign companies registered in Singapore but permitted under their originating jurisdiction to issue those same types of bearer instruments.' FATF and APG (2016), *Anti-money laundering and counter-terrorist financing measures-Singapore*, Fourth Round Mutual Evaluation Report, FATF, Paris and APG, Sydney at 117.

23 See, Emile van der Does de Willebois, Emily M Halter, Robert A Harrison, Ji Won Park, J.C. Sharman, 'The Puppet Masters: How the Corrupt Use Legal Structures to Hide Stolen Assets and What to Do About It' (2011) at 42, World Bank: <https://openknowledge.world-bank.org/bitstream/handle/10986/2363/9780821388945.pdf?sequence=6&isAllowed=y>

24 The use by the OECD and the FATF of the term 'corporate vehicle' to describe a trust is misleading and, in many ways, unfortunate. By referring to them as 'corporate vehicles' or 'legal entities' the uninformed reader is left with the impression that they have the same status in law as a company or some other form of independent status.

25 In France, a 'fiducie' is a contractual arrangement with some elements similar to a trust.

other civil law countries do not recognise trusts at all.

Many trust rules were developed in courts of equity in England over hundreds of years. However, not all the rules are the same today among common law countries due to unique circumstances in each country. The *Hague Convention on the Law Applicable to Trusts and on their Recognition 1985*, while not fully comprehensive in its definition of a trust, provides a basic starting point for describing the elements of a trust. Under Article 2 of that convention, (to paraphrase) a trust refers to a legal relationship created by one person, the settlor, who places assets under the control of another person, the trustee, for the benefit of a third person, the beneficiary. The assets held by the trustee are not part of the trustee's own assets even though legal title to those assets stands in the name of the trustee.[26] The trustee has the power and duty to manage, employ or dispose of the assets in accordance with the terms of the trust and other duties imposed by law.

Trusts serve a variety of legitimate purposes including estate and tax planning, asset protection, wealth management and others. For instance, the parents of a mentally disabled child may establish an income trust for that child's benefit throughout their life to ensure that the child receives a regular income for personal support and maintenance from capital that the child is incapable of managing themselves. But given the nature of trusts, they are capable of being and have been exploited by criminals to hide illicit assets and the domestic and cross-border movement thereof. Some of the vulnerabilities of trusts include the following:

- written instruments are not legally required to settle a trust;
- once settled the settlor's name is removed from ownership of the trust assets;
- it is difficult to determine who the real owner of a trust arrangement is;
- in some cases, such as a discretionary trust, it may be difficult to determine who the beneficiaries of a trust are; and
- in most jurisdictions, there are no requirements to register trusts in any central office.[27]

In the criminal context this means that the recipient of criminal proceeds can shift those proceeds to a trustee concealing his or her name with no written instrument discoverable in criminal investigations or civil proceedings.

A discretionary trust is one where the beneficiaries do not have a fixed entitlement or interest in the property subject to the trust. The trustee of a discretionary trust has

---

Similarly in Luxemburg there exists a 'fiduciary contract'.

26 One of the purposes of the Hague Trust Convention was to deal with conflict of laws issues between civil and common law jurisdictions.

27 There are exceptions to this. For instance, some common law countries require registration in land registries or land titles offices of trust deeds that relate to real property. In South Africa there is a general requirement to register all trusts.

discretion to determine from a range of persons who may be considered beneficiaries to receive capital and income from the trust and how much each may receive. As stated by the Hon Justice Paul Brereton:

> … a discretionary trust does not have beneficiaries in the traditional sense, whose interests together aggregate the beneficial ownership of the trust property. Instead, there is a class of persons, usually described in wide terms, who are the objects of a power to appoint either income or corpus or both to selected members of the class. The members of the class are objects of a power, rather than beneficiaries in the strict sense.[28]

Once the trustee's discretion is exercised in favour of certain persons then those persons are beneficiaries of the trust and not before. For instance, if a person who is a possible beneficiary of the trust is insolvent, the trustee may decide not to exercise his or her discretion to pay any capital or income from the trust. In this type of trust even the beneficiaries are difficult to identify as identification is based on a specified event in time. The potential for abuse by criminals to avoid disclosing beneficiaries is evident. The lack of a certainty to beneficiaries and the power to appoint them by the trustee or another party is a particular vulnerability. As one author commented: '[the assets of a discretionary trust] sit in a kind of ownerless limbo: given away, legally speaking, but without a recipient, so long as the beneficiaries are not defined. Trustees can be guided by a 'letter of wishes', which may allow the settlor to control assets even though legally they do not belong to him.'[29]

In a 2010 FATF report it was noted that trusts can be established in civil law countries that do not recognise trusts by establishing the trust in that civil law country under a foreign law which does recognise trusts.[30] The foreign country under whose laws the trust is established may have a lacuna in their laws which allows the trustee, or the service provider who created the trust, to avoid oversight or supervision by both regulators and law enforcement agencies. This type of lacuna on both sides of the jurisdictional equation is a vulnerability that criminals/money launderers capitalise on.[31]

Innovative arrangements relating to trusts have been constructed within certain jurisdictions to capitalise on the unique nature of trusts and to render them (albeit

---

28 Justice Paul Brereton (2010), 'A Trustee's Lot is Not a Happy One', Address to the National Family Law Conference, Canberra, Tuesday, 19 October 2010 at 3, citing *FCT v Vegners* (1989) 90 ALR 547 at 551–2.

29 The Economist, 'Trust, the Weak Link': <https://www.economist.com/news/international/21589462-cleaning-up-trusts-and-similar-entities-will-hurt-money-launderersbut-it-will-need-lot.>.

30 FATF and CFATF 2010, 'Money Laundering Using Trust And Company Service Providers 2010'.

31 Id at 46.

unintentionally) more vulnerable to criminal exploitation. For instance, in the Cook Islands' mutual evaluation report conducted by the APG in 2009 it was noted that with respect to international trusts established under the *International Trust Act 1984*:

- a trust deed may contain a choice of laws whereby different aspects of the trust may be governed by laws of different jurisdictions; and
- a change in the governing law of an international trust may also be triggered upon 'the occurrence of a specified event'.

A 'specified event' could include political and/or financial uncertainty, breakdown of law and order in the place in which the trust is administered, changes in the law relating to taxation or 'any enquiry' into the trust itself by law enforcement authorities in the jurisdiction where the trust property or trustee is located. In either case, the trust 'flees' the jurisdiction to another.[32] While these types of clauses are not easy to give effect to[33] they may be attractive to criminals to include in trust instruments where jurisdictions (like the Cook Islands) have secrecy provisions in law that forbid the disclosure of any information to third parties in relation to trust assets or beneficial ownership information.

Complex corporate and trust structures

Many corporate structures involve a number of ownership layers, foreign companies and companies owned by trusts through nominee shareholders across multiple jurisdictions. For legitimate multinational companies there may be a number of reasons for this kind of complexity, such as foreign subsidiary operations, corporate mergers/acquisitions and tax advantages. Legitimate arrangements across a number of jurisdictions will almost certainly involve the use of cross-border channels to facilitate wider corporate business programmes.

Obscuring ownership within complex arrangements and exploiting the money flow avenues to move funds are attractive to criminals. A 2006 FATF typologies' report[34] on companies and trusts cites a case where an individual established an international structure with onshore and offshore companies and trusts to commit large-scale fraud. The person purchased insurance companies through a trust and drained the assets of those companies by transferring company funds into accounts in and out of the United States via wire transfers to a corporation he established in

---

32 APG and OGBS, 2009, *Cook Islands Second Round Mutual Evaluation Report*, Sydney at 157.

33 See, for instance, Alexander Bove (2008) 'The Flee Clause: A siren song of asset protection trusts': <https://www.bovelanga.com/~bovelanga/wp-content/uploads/trustworthyadvisor/The%20Flee%20Clause.pdf>.

34 FATF (2006), 'The Misuse of Corporate Vehicles, Including Trust and Company Service Providers 2006'.

the United States. Funds were transferred to an offshore bank account in the name of another corporation that he also controlled. Once the funds were deposited into the offshore bank account, he then used them to pay personal expenses. He laundered approximately USD 225 million over nine years using these structures.[35] Also, the use of corporate directors and the chain of ownership and control is so obscured that it is almost, if not, impossible to determine who owns and control the arrangements.

Complex arrangements across multiple jurisdictions, such as the one cited above, are not difficult to establish and can be rendered more opaque where the structure deliberately employs offshore jurisdictions which have strict corporate or trust secrecy laws.[36] A 2009 report by Global Witness details a number of cases in this regard in which the failings of some banks to comply with their own anti-money laundering policies and so an inability to determine beneficial ownership of corporate clients. [37]

FATF Standards

One of the primary objectives of the FATF recommendations is to ensure that countries or financial and non-financial institutions that do business with companies and trusts, have policies and mechanisms in place to collect information about beneficial owners and have that information available to law enforcement authorities, including foreign counterparts, when conducting criminal investigations.

Before discussing the technical and effectiveness requirements of the FATF standards four key definitions are used by the FATF: [38]

Legal Persons

The term 'legal persons' refers to entities other than natural persons that can establish a permanent customer relationship with a financial institution or own property. They include companies, bodies corporate, foundations, *anstalt*, limited partnerships, or associations. There may be other forms of legal persons in a jurisdiction that fit within this definition (perhaps formed under a statutory instrument). This definition

---

35 Id, case 2 at 4.

36 Vanuatu international companies are particularly attractive to criminals given prohibitions exist in the *International Companies Act* punishable by imprisonment on disclosure of information about the shareholding, beneficial ownership, management, business, affairs, financial affairs or transactions of the company by any person except under a court order. See APG (2015), *Vanuatu Third Round Mutual Evaluation Report*, at 88.

37 Global Witness (2009), 'Undue Diligence: How banks do business with corrupt regimes': <https://www.globalwitness.org>.

38 The definitions summarised here are found in the FATF recommendations and the assessment methodology in the Glossary of *The FATF Recommendations* document.

does not include sole proprietorships or general partnerships. It is aimed only at entities that have an independent legal personality and can enter into binding legal arrangements.

Trust

The terms 'trust' and 'trustee' are defined with reference to the requirements of Article 2 of the *Hague Convention on the Law Applicable to Trusts and their Recognition* which provides that:

> A trust has the following characteristics:
> (a) the assets constitute a separate fund and are not a part of the trustee's own estate;
> (b) title to the trust assets stands in the name of the trustee or in the name of another person on behalf of the trustee;
> (c) the trustee has the power and the duty, in respect of which he is accountable, to manage, employ or dispose of the assets in accordance with the terms of the trust and the special duties imposed upon him by law.

This definition basically captures the nature of trusts in common law countries (like Australia and New Zealand). Various forms of trusts may exist in those jurisdictions such as trusts expressly created to hold or manage assets and trusts implied by the operation of law (e.g., constructive trust or resulting trust). The FATF's concern is with the former.

Beneficial Owner

The term 'beneficial owner' refers to a natural person who ultimately owns or controls a legal person and/or the natural person on whose behalf a transaction is conducted. The term also includes a natural person who exercises ultimate effective control over a legal arrangement or trust. Note that the term includes not just the ultimate owner, but the ultimate controller. Hence, 'beneficial owner' may refer to someone who is not necessarily an owner despite the use of the term 'owner'. This may cause confusion when talking about the beneficial owner of a trust (discussed below).

The FATF also defines two related terms: 'basic ownership information' and 'beneficial ownership information.'[39] The former refers to readily available information such as the natural person who is recorded on a shareholder register or in a corporate registry office as a director, while the latter refers to more complex information including the owners of shareholders which are themselves companies or trusts and in turn may be owned by other companies or trusts (whether foreign

---

39 See FATF Interpretive Note to recommendation 24, Parts A and B respectively.

or domestic). The primary focus of concern is with beneficial ownership information beyond what is termed basic. In many cases beneficial ownership information will not be readily available.

Beneficiary

The term 'beneficiary' refers to the person or persons who are entitled to the benefit of any trust arrangement. The definition is not the same as 'beneficial owner,' although they can be confused. If the beneficiary of a trust is a legal person, the beneficial owner of the trust may be the natural person who ultimately owns or controls that legal person. During FATF consultations with the private sector in 2011 trust practitioners suggested using more accurate terminology than 'beneficial owner' when referring to those who *own* or *control* a trust (trustee) and those who *benefit* from a trust (beneficiaries).[40] But this proposal was not accepted.

Shortly after the startling revelations of the Panama Papers in mid-2016 it was revealed in the Australian media that the Australian Tax Office had approximately 800 persons under investigation with links to the Panamanian law firm named in the papers.[41] According to those media reports, Australian authorities were seeking information from some of the jurisdictions where the companies and trusts had been formed, but were frustrated in receiving beneficial ownership information from those jurisdictions because of secrecy laws or legal professional privilege. However, based on the joint FATF and APG-2015 report on Australia's compliance with the international standards[42], it is likely that should similar requests have been made to Australian authorities in different circumstances, that Australian authorities would not have been in any better position to provide the information requested, even if it wanted to.

The discussion below will first focus on the requirements of those standards and the section following will review how well countries are doing in complying with those requirements, and in effectively mitigating their money laundering risks through companies and trusts.

Technical Requirements

FATF recommendation 24 applies in relation to companies and requires that:

---

40 FATF (2011), 'Compilation of Responses from DNFBPs' submission of Society of Trust and Estate Practitioners (STEP) at 89.

41 <https://www.smh.com.au/business/the-economy/australians-with-links-to-panama-pa-pers-could-be-charged-following-raids-this-week-20160906-gr9sl0.html>.

42 FATF and APG (2015), *Anti-money laundering and counter-terrorist financing measures-Australia,* Fourth Round Mutual Evaluation Report, FATF, Paris and APG, Sydney.

- adequate, accurate and timely information on the beneficial ownership and control of legal persons is kept;
- the above information can be obtained or accessed in a timely fashion by competent authorities;
- effective mitigating measures are in place to address the risk of money laundering and terrorist financing through bearer shares, bearer-share warrants, nominee shareholders and nominee directors; and
- countries consider measures to facilitate access to beneficial ownership and control information by financial institutions and DNFBPs.

An Interpretative Note to recommendation 24 provides that there are two forms of information: basic and beneficial ownership information. Basic information is the rudimentary information about companies or legal persons including the name of the company, its registered office and who its directors are. For beneficial ownership information, countries should have laws in place requiring that either the information on the beneficial ownership of a company is obtained by that company and available at a specified location in their country, or there are mechanisms in place so that the beneficial ownership of a company can be determined in a timely manner by a competent authority.

Some of the problems that were encountered in the last round of evaluations relate to the ability of companies to have information available on the ultimate beneficial owner where there are multiple layers of ownership in a number of companies across a number of jurisdictions. In those situations the ability to go beyond what is held domestically was, and remains, a challenge. This issue was recognised to some extent as a 'lesson-learned' from the previous round of reports. The current requirement now recognises that companies can take reasonable measures to obtain and hold up-to-date information on company beneficial ownership and/or use existing information held by financial and non-financial institutions, government authorities and information available on public companies.[43]

In March 2016 the United Kingdom enacted measures[44] introducing a public register of company beneficial ownership requiring registered companies in the United Kingdom to provide information in the public register on persons with a significant controlling interest in the company.[45] However, British overseas

---

43 Assessment Methodology 2013, R. 24.6(b) and (c), at 65.

44 *Companies Act* 2006 (UK) Part 21A and Schedules 1A and 1B, and Register of People with Significant Control Regulations 2016.

45 The rules came into force on 6 April 2016, requiring companies to have a PSC ('Persons with Significant Controlling Interest') Register. Additional measures came into force on 30 June 2016, which require PSC information to be filed at Companies House as part of the entity's confirmation statement. An individual with significant control is someone who meets at least one of the following five conditions: (1) directly or indirectly hold more than 25% of the nominal share capital; or (2) directly or indirectly control more than 25% of the votes at general meetings; or (3) directly or indirectly be able to control the appointment

territories (notorious as off-shore tax havens) are not required to have such registries. In April 2016 the European Union also took steps to enhance the accessibility of beneficial ownership information through a registry similar to the United Kingdom's.[46]

FATF recommendation 25 applies in relation to trusts and requires that countries:

- have measures to prevent the misuse of legal arrangements for money laundering or terrorist financing,
- ensure that there is adequate, accurate and timely information on express trusts, including information on the settlor, trustee and beneficiaries,
- ensure that this information can be obtained or accessed in a timely fashion by competent authorities,
- consider measures to facilitate access to beneficial ownership and control information by financial institutions and designated non-financial businesses and professions (including trusts and company-service providers).

An Interpretative Note to this recommendation provides that countries should require trustees of express trusts governed under their law to obtain and hold adequate, accurate, and current beneficial ownership information regarding the trust; and the category of persons on whom to gather information is expanded to include a 'protector, if any' and 'any other person exercising ultimate effective control over the trust.'

As pointed at above, the definition of 'beneficial owner' includes the person with ultimate effective control and is referred to in the fourth bullet point, on whom to collect information; and 'beneficiary' is defined in the FATF recommendations[47] differently from 'beneficial owner'.[48]

What is confusing is that, under some of the measures elucidated in the Interpretative Note, countries are required to do things in relation to beneficial owners but not in relation to beneficiaries, and in other measures they are required to do things in relation to both. For instance, the FATF assessment methodology has a confusing requirement that states:

---

or removal of a majority of the board; or (4) actually exercise, or have the right to exercise, significant influence or control over the company; or (5) actually exercise or have the right to exercise significant influence or control over any trust or firm (which is not a legal entity) which has significant control (under one of the four conditions above) over the company.

46 EU (2016) 'Proposal for a Directive Of The European Parliament And Of The Council': <http://ec.europa.eu/justice/criminal/document/files/aml-directive_en.pdf>.

47 Id Glossary at 146.

48 Id at 147.

25.1 Countries should require:
(a) trustees of any express trust governed under their law to obtain and hold adequate, accurate, and current information on the identity of the settlor, the trustee(s), the protector (if any), the beneficiaries or class of beneficiaries, and any other natural person exercising ultimate effective control over the trust.

Trustees under this requirement must collect current information on beneficiaries (as defined), which can be legal persons, not necessarily natural persons, who are entitled to the benefit of the trust. But the requirement does not extend further to any natural person (i.e. shareholder who is a beneficial owner) beyond the legal person. The requirement in the last phrase, to 'collect information on the natural person who exercises ultimate effective control' is only with respect to the natural person who controls the trust but does not beneficially own the trust property. In other words and to be concise, in a trust arrangement there is no requirement to collect information on the natural person who ultimately owns the property administered in a trust. There does not appear to be a rationale for the difference and this has led to some degree of confusion as to how to apply and assess recommendation 25 for any given country.

Moreover, an often missed point in this recommendation is the creation of a regulatory gap resulting from the wording 'governed under their laws' (see above). This wording means that a trustee, and the assets he, she or it manages, located in one jurisdiction but whose trust is governed under the laws of another jurisdiction (i.e. a foreign trust) is not required under the jurisdiction in which he or she is located to comply with any local requirements to hold accurate information. The foreign law, which may or may not have that requirement, would apply. However, even if it did have the same requirement, how the governing law could be enforced is a good question.[49] Under a recent guidance note issued by the FATF,[50] in the case of countries where foreign trusts are formed, but whose laws do not recognise domestic trust arrangements, a number of the requirements in recommendation 25 still apply but do not address this issue. In particular, it provides that trustees must be required to disclose their status to financial institutions and non-financial businesses when forming a business relationship or carrying out an occasional transaction. The trustee needs to actively make such disclosure and not only upon the request of a competent authority.[51] Also, professional trustees must maintain

---

49 FATF (2011), 'Compilation of Responses from DNFBPs' id at 98. Despite objections made to the FATF in relation to this recommendation by trust lawyers and practitioners, no changes were made to the wording. 'Most practitioners, however, would argue that such an arrangement is unrealistic and likely to be ineffective. It would be preferable instead for trustees' residence … to be the basis of regulatory responsibility for a trust.'

50 FATF (2014), 'Transparency and Beneficial Ownership Information 2014'.

51 Trustees should not be prevented from doing this even if, for example, the terms of the trust deed require them to conceal their status. The only source of information on the trust-

the information they hold for at least five years after their involvement with the trust ceases.

Effective Implementation

In the last round of evaluations from 2003 to 2012 it became clear to the FATF, APG and other assessor bodies that while many countries issued laws and regulations to comply with the technical requirements of the FATF recommendations, the use of those laws to mitigate money-laundering and terrorist-financing risk, and to address it when it occurred, was lacking in the majority of countries. This was not entirely the fault of the countries themselves, however. The FATF standards, including the assessment methodology, lacked a clear set of policy objectives and criteria to judge whether a country was effective in addressing its risk. It was therefore decided in 2013, to address this issue and include a set of effectiveness criteria in the FATF's assessment methodology.

In 2013 the FATF agreed on a set of eleven 'immediate outcomes,' within a larger framework of three intermediate outcomes and a higher level objective, to judge effective implementation of the FATF standards. According to the FATF, '[in] the AML/CFT context, effectiveness is the extent to which financial systems and economies mitigate the risks and threats of money laundering, and financing of terrorism and proliferation. This could be in relation to the intended result of a given (a) policy, law, or enforceable means; (b) programme of law enforcement, supervision, or intelligence activity; or (c) implementation of a specific set of measures to mitigate the money-laundering and financing of terrorism risks, and combat the financing of proliferation'.[52]

Each of the eleven immediate outcomes contains within itself, an overarching policy objective and a set of criteria to judge whether a country is achieving the objective. Immediate Outcome 5 (IO 5) relates to companies and trusts. The policy objective of IO 5 is as follows: 'legal persons and arrangements are prevented from misuse for money laundering or terrorist financing, and information on their beneficial ownership is available to competent authorities without impediments.' A set of mandatory core issues accompanies the defined outcome which assessors are expected to apply to a country. Those core issues are the following.[53]

> 5.1 To what extent is the information on the creation and types of legal persons and arrangements in the country available publicly?
>
> 5.2 How well do the relevant competent authorities identify, assess and

---

ee often available comes from the business relationship of a financial institution/DNFBP and the trustee.

52 Assessment Methodology 2013 at 15.

53 Id at 103–4.

understand the vulnerabilities, and the extent to which legal persons created in the country can be, or are being misused for (money laundering and terrorist financing) 'ML/TF'?

5.3   How well has the country implemented measures to prevent the misuse of legal persons and arrangements for ML/TF purposes?

5.4   To what extent can relevant competent authorities obtain adequate, accurate and current basic and beneficial ownership information on all types of legal persons created in the country, in a timely manner?

5.5   To what extent can relevant competent authorities obtain adequate, accurate and current beneficial ownership information on legal arrangements, in a timely manner?

5.6   To what extent are effective, proportionate and dissuasive sanctions applied against persons who do not comply with the information requirements?

One thing that is likely to jump out at the reader is how, or even whether, it is possible to form a view that companies and trusts have been prevented from being used for money laundering and terrorist financing (the overall objective) even if the answers to all six questions in the above are favourable to the country under assessment. Can such answers prove a negative? That's doubtful. Positive answers to the first two questions above (5.1 and 5.2) cannot contribute to that understanding. Just because information is available and competent authorities understand specific risks cannot, of itself, achieve the goal of preventing money laundering and terrorist financing. A positive answer to core issues 5.4 and 5.5 (to what extent can authorities get information and to what extent they impose effective sanctions) is also of dubious value in judging whether criminals have been prevented from exploiting companies and trusts for illicit purposes.

That leaves core issue 5.3. In many ways, core issue 5.3 simply asks in a roundabout way the very question that is the goal of IO 5. However, it is not helpful to ask whether a specific country achieves an objective by asking whether that country has achieved the relevant objective.

Snapshot of Compliance so far

Australia was one of the first countries to be evaluated under the new FATF standards. The report of that evaluation, published in April 2015, revealed that Australia lacks a clear process for obtaining or recording company beneficial ownership information and that there is no mechanism to ensure that information on company registers is accurate. More importantly, Australian law does not require companies or company registers to obtain and hold up-to-date information to determine the ultimate natural person who is the beneficial owner beyond the immediate shareholder. Nor are companies required to take reasonable measures to obtain and hold that information. With respect to Australian trust law, the 2015 report noted that there is no obligation for trustees to hold and maintain information on trusts and what information trustees do keep is not required to be up to date and accurate.

Results for other countries reflected in FATF, APG and other assessor body reports since 2012 are also not impressive. Below is a table of compliance levels of all reports published from 2012 to October 2017.[54] A rating of NC or PC on technical compliance for recommendations 24 and 25 is considered an unsatisfactory rating. A rating of low or moderate on effectiveness is also considered unsatisfactory. Thirty-eight countries have been assessed so far and only four countries have received satisfactory ratings in all three categories.

Table of Compliance Levels* (as at October 2017)			
Countries	R. 24 Companies	R. 25 Trusts	IO 5 Effectiveness
1. Australia	PC	NC	Moderate
2. Canada	PC	NC	Low
3. Malaysia	PC	PC	Moderate
4. Singapore	PC	PC	Moderate
5. United States	NC	PC	Low
6. Bangladesh	PC	PC	Low
7. Bhutan	PC	LC	Low
8. Fiji	PC	PC	Low
9. Samoa	PC	PC	Moderate
10. Sri Lanka	NC	NC	Low
11. Vanuatu	NC	NC	Low
12. Austria	PC	PC	Moderate
13. Belgium	LC	LC	Moderate
14. Italy	LC	LC	Substantial
15. Norway	PC	PC	Moderate
16. Spain	LC	LC	Substantial
17. Switzerland	LC	LC	Moderate

---

54 The countries listed here have been evaluated by either FATF, APG, other FSRBs, the World Bank or the IMF.

* NC: Non-compliant; PC: Partially complaint; LC: Largely compliant; C: Compliant; NA: Not applicable Low: Low effectiveness: Moderate: Moderately effective; Substantial: Substantially effective; High: Highly effective.

18. Ethiopia	PC	NA	Moderate
19. Jamaica	PC	PC	Low
20. Guatemala	LC	LC	Moderate
21. Trinidad and Tobago	PC	PC	Moderate
22. Uganda	NC	NC	Low
23. Zimbabwe	NC	NC	Low
24. Costa Rica	PC	PC	Low
25. Cuba	LC	C	Substantial
26. Honduras	NC	LC	Low
27. Tunisia	PC	NC	Low
28. Armenia	LC	LC	Substantial
29. Hungary	PC	PC	Low
30. Serbia	LC	PC	Moderate
31. Isle of Man	PC	PC	Moderate
32. Sweden	PC	PC	Moderate
33. Cambodia	PC	PC	Moderate
34. Ireland	LC	PC	Substantial
35. Slovenia	LC	LC	Moderate
36. Mongolia	PC	PC	Low
37. Denmark	PC	PC	Moderate
38. Bahamas	PC	PC	Low

Satisfactory ratings for technical compliance do not mean a system is effective. Likewise, while the FATF has indicated on many occasions that low compliance levels for technical compliance does not necessarily mean that a system cannot receive a passing mark on effectiveness that has not, as yet, occurred.

Of the thirty-eight countries assessed to October 2017, only four countries (Italy, Spain, Cuba and Armenia), received satisfactory ratings in all three categories. Of those that received satisfactory ratings for technical compliance with recommendations 24 and 25 some received unsatisfactory rating for effective implementation (Belgium, Switzerland, and Guatemala). Hence, while they have taken the time and effort to meet the technical requirements of those standards they fail to effectively implement those measures and in doing so fail to effectively mitigate their risk of money laundering through companies and trusts.

Some of the common deficiencies noted in reports so far include the following:

Common Deficiencies		
R. 24 Companies	R. 25 Trusts	IO 5 Effectiveness
• Failure to undertake risk assessments for all types of legal persons.	• No obligation on trustees to hold and maintain information on trusts.	• Authorities do not understand the risk related to companies and trusts.
• No mechanisms to ensure information on company registers is accurate. • No process for obtaining or recording company beneficial ownership information. • Financial institutions do not verify beneficial ownership information. • No disclosure obligations extant for nominee shareholders and nominee directors. • Where bearer shares and bearer-share warrants are permitted there are no measures in place to address money-laundering risk. • Limited partnerships and other forms of legal persons are not covered.	• No obligation for trustees to keep information up to date and accurate. • Trustees are not required to disclose their status to financial institutions when carrying out a financial transaction for the trust. • Reliance on CDD by reporting entities means that beneficial ownership information is not always available with foreign trusts. • Lack of proportionate and dissuasive sanctions to enforce requirement to exchange information. • Information on trusts held by tax authorities not available to law enforcement.	• Information on the creation and types of legal arrangements, including trusts, is not publicly available. • Access to beneficial ownership by government authorities is not timely. • Beneficial ownership information is not used. • Law enforcement does not pay adequate attention to the potential misuse of legal entities or trusts, in particular in cases of complex structures. • Beneficial ownership information for foreign legal persons or arrangements is not available for criminal investigations.

Many of the countries listed above that received unsatisfactory ratings for recommendations 24 and 25 were marked with the same unsatisfactory ratings and same deficiencies in the previous round of evaluations from 2003 to 2012. It is therefore disappointing that corrective action had not been taken, in some cases, after a considerable number of years especially in light of the significant vulnerabilities posed by the nature of companies and trusts. Given the increased focus by the G-20 on beneficial ownership and the continuing revelations not just from the Panama papers but other revelations, what action the FATF and other bodies may take to address this inaction will be interesting to watch.

Conclusion

The Panama paper revelations in early 2016 and the G-20 statement on beneficial ownership issues in the same year have now increased attention on the widespread criminal abuse of company and trust structures, and on the need to address beneficial ownership issues well beyond technical experts to the wider public. The anonymous hacker who leaked the papers to the German media outlet, Süddeutsche Zeitung which, in turn, disclosed data to the International Consortium of Investigative Journalists, citing the abuse of shell companies, tax evasion and political corruption, stated that one of the reasons he or she leaked the information was because of 'income inequality … one of the defining issues of our time … The debate over its sudden acceleration has raged for years, with politicians, academics and activists alike helpless to stop its steady growth despite countless speeches, statistical analyses, a few meagre protests, and the occasional documentary.'[55]

There is no doubt that company and trust structures pose considerable risks for money laundering and terrorist financing. The FATF's standards have focused on these issues from the outset in 1989 but more closely after 2003 and more intensively since 2012. It is disappointing therefore that, with almost 30 years since the FATF's establishment, serious efforts to mitigate money-laundering and terrorist-financing risks (as discussed in the previous chapter) through the exploitation of companies and trusts have continued to lag by most countries. Unless serious efforts are undertaken to implement the minimum requirements of the FATF standards, despite some ambiguities and anomalies within those standards, criminals will continue to exploit the weaknesses inherent in company and trust structures to achieve their goals of maximizing criminal profits and using those profits to reinvest in further criminal activity.

---

55 John Doe (2016), 'The Revolution Will Be Digitized': <https://panamapapers.icij. org/20160506-john-doe-statement.html>.

Chapter 9

The Law Enforcement Implications of the Panama Papers

Dr David Chaikin

Background

From early 2015 to April 2016 a mysterious and anonymous person called 'John Doe', who had access to the internal files of Mossack Fonesca (Mossfon), released a huge cache of documents to Bastian Obermayer and Frederik Obermaier, investigative journalists with the German newspaper, Süddeutsche Zeitung. The 11.5 million documents known as the Panama Papers included the records of 214,000 offshore companies, foundations and trusts which Mossfon had established on behalf of its clients since 1977.[1] The scale of this theft (or leakage) was so great that Süddeutsche Zeitung partnered with the International Consortium of Investigative Journalists (ICIJ), which entered into access arrangements with 400 journalists from over 100 media organisations in 76 countries. The investigative journalists mined the database, carrying out secret investigations for nearly a year prior to the publication of a torrent of articles in April 2016.[2] The world's leading newspapers accused Panama and other offshore jurisdictions of aiding and abetting corrupt politicians, money launderers and wealthy tax evaders.[3] The news media also criticised the intermediaries, particularly banks and law firms, which had purchased corporate entities on behalf of their clients, with scant regard to the potential misuse of such entities. Much of the journalistic focus was directed at Mossfon, a leading law firm in Panama and the fourth largest trust and company service provider (TCSP) in the world, raising important issues as to the role of law firms and TCSPs in facilitating international financial crime.

This was not the first ICIJ journalistic exposé based on stolen documents from a TCSP. In 2015 in the Offshore Leaks scandal, ICIJ journalists carried out an investigation into 2.5 million files concerning 120,000 offshore companies which had been stolen from the Singapore-based TCSP, Portcullis TrustNet, and the

---

1 Bastian Obermayer and Frederik Obermaier, *The Panama Papers: Breaking the Story of How the Rich & Powerful Hide their Money* (2017), One World.

2 See BTG Global Advisory, *Paper Chase* (2016).

3 See for example, Liam Stack, Steven Erlanger, Bryant Rousseau, Michael Forsythe, Neil MacFarquhar and Stephen Castle, 'What are the Panama Papers?' *New York Times* (5 April 2016); and 'The Panama papers: a torrential leak'), *The Economist* (9 April 2016).

British Virgin Islands-based TCSP, Commonwealth Trust Limited (CTL). The ICIJ journalists revealed that the Anti-Money Laundering (AML) regulator in the British Virgin Islands had accused CTL of systematically breaching AML laws 'between 2003 and 2008 by failing to verify and record its client identities and backgrounds'.[4] Similarly in the Panama Papers, the journalists have highlighted the extensive manipulation of corporate secrecy, through concealment of beneficial ownership by the world's political and economic elite.

In the next sections, I will analyse the type of clients that Mossfon serviced and question whether Mossfon discharged its legal responsibilities under global AML standards.

Mossfon and its Clients

The principal line of business of Mossfon is the sale of companies and trusts to institutional intermediaries, such as banks, law firms, accounting practices, brokers, asset managers and specialist financial advisors. For the most part Mossfon was not in the trust services or asset management business, but was a wholesale supermarket for offshore corporate entities. With 45 offices throughout the world, including 10 in China, Mossfon serviced a wide geographical spread of clients. Mossfon's client base consisted of 14,153 intermediaries from over 100 countries, with intermediaries from Hong Kong, Switzerland and the United Kingdom (UK) requesting the largest number of trusts and companies.[5] The sheer size of the number of intermediaries shows that there is a very large global market for offshore companies and trusts and that offshore corporate structures are an essential feature of global business and finance. Although the intermediaries may have used some of the corporate entities for their own internal purposes, the overwhelming majority of corporate entities were used by their customers (the 'end-clients' in Mossfon's terminology).[6]

According to the investigative journalists associated with the Panama Papers, the ultimate clients of Mossfon included:

> one hundred and forty politicians and public officials around the world, including the prime ministers of Iceland and Pakistan, the king of Saudi Arabia, the president of Ukraine, persons associated with the president of Russia and various Chinese politicians, as well as a number of ministers

---

4 Gerard Ryle, Marina Walker Guevara, Michael Hudson, Nicky Hager, Duncan Campbell and Stefan Candea, 'Secret Files Expose Offshore's Global Impact'. *International Consortium of Investigative Journalists* (3 April 2013): <https://www.icij.org/offshore/secret-files-expose-offshores-global-impact>.

5 Rigoberto Carvajal, Mar Cabra, Álvaro Ortiz and Fernando Blat 'Explore the Panama Papers Key Figures'. *International Consortium of Investigative Journalists*: <https://panamapapers.icij.org/graphs/>.

6 Bastian Obermayer and Frederik Obermaier, above n1 at 148–9.

and politicians from Argentina, Azerbaijan, Brazil, Ecuador, France and Nigeria. The Panama Papers have led directly to the resignation of the prime minister of Iceland and provided the impetus for an investigation in Pakistan, which culminated in an order by the Supreme Court in Pakistan disqualifying the incumbent prime minister. In some cases, such as the offshore corporate vehicle associated with the current prime minister of Australia, the information is rather dated in that it concerns a time when the prime minister was a businessman and not a politician, with no suggestion that there was anything untoward in the conduct of the prime minister;

more than 33 individuals and companies who are the subject of the US Department of Treasury Office of Foreign Asset Control's sanctions including drug kingpins, terrorist groups and 'rogue states', such as North Korea;

nearly 30 persons listed in Forbes 500 rich person's list, as well as famous celebrities, movie stars, soccer professionals, some of whom have subsequently been convicted of tax evasion.

Mossfon's Responsibilities in Dealing with its Clients

The legal and ethical responsibility of Mossfon for aiding end-clients who misuse corporate vehicles is one of the significant issues arising from the Panama Papers. Mossfon claimed that it did not deal directly with end-clients and that it has no legal or ethical responsibility if some of these end-clients turned out to be 'bad guys'. Indeed, Mossfon has disclaimed any responsibility for the offshore services that it has provided, arguing by analogy that what a person does with a car (company) is not the responsibility of the car manufacturer (trust and company service provider).[7] This is a simplistic analogy that is not appropriate, given that a TCSP is required under global AML standards to know the identity of the ultimate beneficial owner of a corporate vehicle. It also ignores how important TCSPs are in facilitating crimes such as fraud; it has been held in some common law jurisdictions that a TCSP which provides a secrecy structure to an unknown client faces the risk of civil liability if it turns out that that client is using secrecy to conceal a fraud from a third party and launders the proceeds of that fraud.[8]

The claim by Mossfon that it is ignorant of the activities of end-clients should not be accepted at face value. According to Obermayer and Obermaier, although 'Mossfon usually knows very little about these [end-client] people', it was well aware of the reasons why the intermediaries needed particular types of shell companies,

---

7 See *Bastian Obermayer, Gerard Ryle, Marina Walker Guevara, Michael Hudson & Ors*, 'Giant Leak of Offshore Financial Records Exposes Global Array of Crime and Corruption'. *International Consortium of Investigative Journalists* (3 April 2016): <https://panamapapers. icij.org/20160403-panama-papers-global-overview.html>.

8 See *Agip (Africa) Ltd* v *Jackson* [1990] EWCA Civ 2 (The accountants who provide a series of shell companies to a fraudster were held liable under the constructive trust doctrine).

and even advised as to which tax-haven company structure would be most suitable for the end-client's objectives.[9] Further, there is evidence that employees of Mossfon knew the identity of and worked directly with a number of dubious end-clients.[10]

The subsequent law enforcement raids on the offices of Mossfon in Panama and elsewhere indicate that Mossfon was in possession of documentation that might be important in any criminal investigation of Mossfon and its clients. In February 2017 the founders of Mossfon, Jürgen Mossack and Ramon Fonseca, were arrested and denied bail in circumstances where Mossfon was accused of being a potential 'criminal organization' that concealed and removed evidence related to 'illegal activity.'[11] In particular, it was alleged that Mossfon had facilitated the systematic laundering of bribe monies through providing offshore corporate vehicles and bank accounts in connection with a major Brazilian corruption scandal (Operation Car Wash). The Panama prosecutor accused the Brazilian operations of Mossfon of 'offer[ing] financial products aimed at hiding money that entered the Panamanian financial system', while the defence counsel of Mr Mossack and Mr Fonesca has argued that the bank accounts were not laundering vehicles but were the recipients of legal administrative fees owed to Mossfon.[12]

The arrest of Mossfon founders has had a significant impact on Mossfon, with many of its customers abandoning the firm. By August 2017, 39 of Mossfon's 45 overseas offices were closed, including its offices in Jersey, Gibraltar, the Isle of Man and Luxembourg. In the British Virgin Islands, an administrator was appointed to oversee its operations and report to the local regulator. In the United States the local affiliates of Mossfon in Wyoming and Nevada have gone out of business, after resigning as registered agents, with MF Corporate Services (Nevada) agreeing to pay a fine of $10,000 for failing to keep proper records and information about its clients. In Panama, Mossack Fonesca Asset Management SA, the financial services arm of Mossfon, was liquidated following an investigation by the corporate securities regulator into potential violations of clients' due diligence requirements.

In the next sections, I assess the utility of the public website of the Panama Papers, and question whether the raw data of the Panama Papers should be made available to law enforcement.

---

9 Bastian Obermayer and Frederik Obermaier, above n1 at 148–9.

10 Id at 43.

11 Will Fitzgibbon, Emilia Díaz-Struck and Michael Hudson, 'Founders of Panama Papers Law Firm Arrested on Money Laundering Charges'. *International Consortium of Investigative Journalists* (11 February 2017): <https://panamapapers.icij.org/20170211-mossfon-pana-ma-arrests.html>.

12 Will Fitzgibbon, 'Panama Claims Solid Case Against Mossack Fonseca'. *International Consortium of Investigative Journalists* (27 March 2017) at 7.

The Public Website of the Panama Papers

One of the reasons that the Panama Papers continues to have a major impact on the public discourse was the decision by ICIJ to create a website containing a large amount of information concerning the Panama Papers. On 9 May 2016 an ICIJ website containing a searchable database of the Panama Papers and other massive leaks (including the Offshore Leaks and the Bahamian leaks) went public. What then can be found in the searchable public database?[13] The database which consists of more than 500,000 corporate entities can be searched either by inserting the name of an individual, company or address, or by inserting the name of a country or jurisdiction. A search of an individual, such as a named officer of a company, will reveal whether that individual is a shareholder or officer in any company on the database, and will produce a visualised map of that individual's connections with other persons in the database.

On 17 September 2017, I visited the Panama Papers website by putting the word 'Australia' in the search engine; 118 offshore entities, 1704 officers, 1408 addresses and 201 intermediaries were identified as linked to Australia. Interestingly, none of the offshore entities were registered in Australia, albeit that there were quite a large number of entities that had an 'undetermined place of incorporation'. This would suggest that Australian shell companies are not attractive to foreign persons. In contrast, 47 New Zealand companies are in the database, and these companies have links to other jurisdictions, such as Brazil, Columbia, Ecuador, Malta, Panama and Peru. Indeed, the Panama Papers referred to New Zealand on more than 61,000 occasions, and one New Zealand accountant was allegedly listed in more than 4,500 documents.[14] Following a public outcry that the Panama Papers showed that New Zealand trusts were being used by foreign tax evaders and money launderers, a New Zealand Government Inquiry into Foreign Trusts was established. The New Zealand government accepted the Shewan Inquiry's recommendations concerning new and stringent foreign-trust disclosure rules, and this has resulted in new legislation which came into effect on 21 February 2017. The impact of the new rules has been dramatic with a mere 3,000 foreign trusts deciding to register with the New Zealand Inland Revenue, with 8,750 foreign trusts deciding not to register, presumably avoiding the risk that beneficial ownership or control information on such trusts may be passed by them to foreign tax authorities.[15]

---

13 International Consortium of Investigative Journalists, *Offshore Leaks Database*: <http://www.cbc.ca/news/business/panama-papers-icij-database-public-search-1.3573622>.

14 Charlotte Greenfield and Rebecca Howard, 'Panama Papers: World's rich use tax-free New Zealand shelf companies to hide funds', *Business Insider* (9 May 2016).

15 John Glover, 'Trusts, tax and transparency: the new reporting obligations', Paper prepared for the *Conference on Use and Abuse of Trusts and Other Wealth Management Devices, Singapore Academy of Law,* Singapore (27 July 2017) at 25 (There were 11,750 foreign trusts as at 30 December 2016).

Should the Panama Papers Database be made available to Law Enforcement or to the Public?

It is important to realise that the database of Mossfon containing the original and underlying documentation found in the Panama Papers has not been released by the ICIJ to law enforcement or to the public. Instead, a stripped-down searchable ICIJ database has been made available to the public, which excludes much of the raw material constituting the Panama Papers. Moreover, the public database does not contain a summary of private and confidential information, such as details about bank accounts, financial transactions, identity documents and email exchanges between employees of Mossfon or between Mossfon and its clients.[16]

Questions have been raised as to whether the entire Panama Papers should be released to law enforcement. Soon after the publication of the database on ICIJ's website in May 2016, a person called 'John Doe', reputedly the source of the Panama Papers, offered to make the documentation available to governments. 'John Doe', in a public statement, argued that by allowing law enforcement agencies access to the Panama Papers, 'thousands of prosecutions' could follow.[17] However, the ICIJ has refused to hand over the Panama Papers to governments because ICIJ is 'not an arm of law enforcement and is not an agent of the government'.[18] This is a curious statement from an organisation that has spearheaded the international agenda for improved transparency in government and the corporate sector. One possible explanation is that the ICIJ does not wish to hand over the database to governments, since it is suspects that some governments are corrupt and will pass the raw material information in the Panama Papers to organised criminals and tax evaders.

This raises a more general issue concerning improved exchanges of information between governments: for example, should there be limits imposed in respect of international co-operation between tax authorities where there are 'black hat' governments who are on the side of the 'bad guys'.[19] How can a government impose limits if the country is a party to the Common Reporting Standard which requires the automatic exchange of information on financial information?

It was reported that ICIJ has resisted supplying the Panama Papers to the US

---

16 See Marina Walker Guevara, 'Coming Soon: ICIJ to Release Panama Papers Offshore Companies Data', *International Consortium of Investigative Journalists* (26 April 2016): <https://panamapapers.icij.org/20160426-database-coming-soon.html>.

17 John Doe, 'The Revolution will be Digitized', *International Consortium of Investigative Journalists* (6 May 2016): <https://panamapapers.icij.org/20160506-john-doe-statement.html>.

18 Marina Walker Guevara, 'Frequently asked questions about ICIJ and the Panama Papers', *International Consortium of Investigative Journalists* (6 April 2016).

19 See William Byrnes, 'How May the United States Leverage its FATCA IGA Bilateral Process to Incentivize Good Tax Administrations among the World of Black Hat and Grey Hat Governments? A Carrot & Stick Policy Proposal', *Emory International Law Review* (13 February 2017), Vol. 31 No. 1, 2017.

Attorney's Office, a reputable US government agency, on the grounds that it was a media company protected by the First Amendment to the US Constitution.[20] However, for those countries that do not enjoy the same constitutional protection for the media, there is a possibility that a domestic government agency could issue a notice requiring the production of such information which could not be successfully resisted by local journalists. It was for this reason that the ICIJ appears to have put in place extraordinary security measures to prevent access by foreign governments to the raw material underlying the Panama Papers. Nevertheless, some governments have received a copy of the entire Panama Papers database. For example, the government of Denmark announced that it had purchased the Panama Papers for £1 million[21], which, if correct, is a very cheap price. New Zealand's Government Inquiry into Foreign Trusts stated that it was not able to access the Panama Papers[22], while the Australian Taxation Office (ATO) appears to have received the entire Panama Papers database from a foreign government(s) without making any payment[23] by relying on its 100 or so tax treaty arrangements.[24] Indeed, the ATO has suggested that it has received eleven 'data sets' (including the Panama Papers) from its overseas tax government partners, thereby confirming the potential utility of stolen (or leaked) data to reduce the asymmetry of information between the ATO and taxpayers. The discussion in the next section pinpoints the value of the Panama Papers to law enforcement agencies and tax authorities.

Impact of Panama Papers on Law Enforcement and Tax Collection

The Panama Papers has had an unprecedented effect on launching and/or consolidating law enforcement and tax investigations throughout the world. The range of significant information found in the Panama Papers is not doubted, with beneficial ownership information providing an avenue for more detailed

20 Alon Kaplan, 'The Panama Papers-Disclosure to Government agencies – Is this possible?' <https://www.linkedin.com/pulse/panama-papers-disclosure-government-agencies-is-dr-alon-kaplan-tep> (1 May 2016).

21 Jason Murdock 'Denmark is the first country to pay £1 million for Panama Papers files to expose tax evaders'. *International Business Times* (7 September 2016).

22 New Zealand Government, *Government Inquiry into Foreign Trust Disclosure Rules*, The Treasury: <http://www.treasury.govt.nz/publications/reviews-consultation/foreign-trust-disclosure-rules> (8 June 2016).

23 See Chris Jordan, the ATO Commissioner, answer to a question contained in the transcript of the joint press conference between The Hon Kelly O'Dwyer MP, Minister for Revenue and Financial Services, and The Hon Michael Keenan MP Minister for Justice Minister Assisting the Prime Minister for Counter Terrorism, Melbourne: <http://kmo.ministers.treasury.gov.au/transcript/050-2016/> (6 September 2016).

24 For a list of Australia's 36 Tax Information Exchange Agreements, see <https://www.ato.gov.au/General/International-tax-agreements/In-detail/Tax-information-exchange-agreements-%28TIEA%29/Tax-information-exchange-agreements---overview/>.

investigations. It has been reported that by December 2016 the Panama Papers had resulted in 'at least 150 investigations in 79 countries and \$110 million recouped by governments so far'.[25] It is not only money laundering and other financial crimes that are being investigated. According to various EU Parliamentary reports, the Panama Papers identified tax avoidance schemes which may have resulted in losses of more than €109 billion in the EU for the year 2015.[26] National governments have established task forces into the Panama Papers, with tax authorities playing a leading role in investigating tax activities of persons mentioned in the Panama Papers. Soon after the Panama Papers were disclosed, the UK Government established a cross-government task force led by HM Revenue & Customs and the National Crime Agency, whose initial investigatory focus has been on 700 persons identified by the Panama Papers.[27]

In response to the Panama Papers, the Australian government, through its Serious Financial Crime Task Force, mounted a 'whole-of-government response', targeting the most important matters raised by the Papers. According to the annual report of the Australian Crime Commission (now called the Australian Criminal Intelligence Commission, ACIC) about 1,000 Australians have been identified through the Panama Papers, and 80 of those persons have been matched to the ACIC's 'criminal intelligence holdings', with some individuals also on the National Criminal Target List.[28] These individuals are alleged to be major criminals, including members of 'serious bikie gangs' and promoters of illicit offshore tax schemes,[29] thereby providing evidence of the attraction of offshore corporate structures to Australian organised crime. Indeed, the ACIC has provided 32 'intelligence products' to Australian law enforcement agency partners through utilising information in the Panama Papers. According to various media reports, the ATO has commenced investigations into more than 800 Australian taxpayers identified in the Panama Papers, with 100 ATO officers making 15 'unannounced visits' in Victoria and Queensland, and search warrants being executed on six accounting firms associated with 60 clients.[30] The

---

25 Will Fitzgibbon and Emilia Díaz-Struck and Michael Hudson, 'Panama Papers Have Had Historic Global Effects – and the Impacts Keep Coming', *International Consortium of Investigative Journalists* (1 December 2016).

26 Vidya Kauri, 'EU Report Says Banks Should Report Tax Avoidance Schemes', *Law360* (25 April 2017).

27 UK Government, 'UK launches cross-government taskforce on the "Panama Papers"' (10 April 2016): <https://www.gov.uk/government/news/uk-launches-cross-government-task-force-on-the-panama-papers>.

28 See Australian Crime Commission, *Annual Report 2015–16* at 70–1.

29 Statement by Michael Kennan, Commissioner of the Australian Federal Police (2016), *Press Conference with Minister of Revenue and Financial Services, and Minister for Justice* (6 September) Melbourne.

30 Interview by Warren Moore with the Hon. Kelly O'Dwyer MP, Minister for Revenue

ATO has also been active in the international front through its chairmanship of the OECD's Joint International Task Force on Shared Intelligence, where the Panama Papers have been a major agenda items for its 30 or more members.[31]

The Panama Papers are likely to be more useful to Australian law enforcement and tax authorities than in other jurisdictions because of the wide ranging mandatory reporting requirement under *Anti-Money Laundering and Counter-Terrorist Financing Act 2006* (Cth). One of the reasons that Australia is in a better position than nearly all onshore jurisdictions to investigate offshore corporate secrets, such as those found in the Panama Papers, is its comprehensive AML reporting system in relation to overseas wire transfers. Since 1992 all financial institutions in Australia have been required to report International Funds Transfer Instructions (IFTIs), both in and out of Australia, and irrespective of their size.[32] These reports which concern hundreds of millions of transactions are captured and stored by AUSTRAC, Australia's Financial Intelligence Unit and AML regulator, and then subject to extensive analysis by AUSTRAC and its partner agencies, particularly the ATO.[33] The Panama Papers have already proved useful, with AUSTRAC finding that $2.5 billion of funds are linked to individuals and corporate entities disclosed by the Panama Papers. Investigations are underway to determine the legitimacy of these funds, but this is a complex task because it relates to a period going back 10 years. Further, AUSTRAC has issued 10 notices to various banks requiring the disclosure of additional information associated with the bank accounts that have been identified as linked to the Panama Papers.

In the next sections, I examine some of the policy implications of the Panama Papers, relating to the regulation of TCSPs and the future role of OFCs.

Regulation of Trust and Company Service Providers under AML laws

One of the important lessons of the Panama Papers is that TCSPs, such as Mossfon, play a critical role in facilitating international financial crime, whether wittingly or unwittingly. This has been recognised by the FATF which revised its global standards on money laundering and terrorist financing (FATF Recommendations) in 2003 to impose gatekeeping responsibilities on TCSPs.

Under the FATF Recommendations, a TCSP is defined as 'all those persons

---

and Financial Services, 2GB Radio Station:< http://www.kellyodwyer.com.au/interview-with-warren-moore-2gb> (8 September 2016).

31 Sean Mullins and Jonathan Slater, 'Mossack Fonseca, Panama and the Implications for Australia', *Clayton Utz* (14 April 2016).

32 *Anti-Money Laundering and Counter-Terrorism Financing Act* 2006 (Cth) ss. 45–6.

33 For the background, see Neil J. Jensen, 'International Funds Transfer Instructions: Australia at the Leading Edge of Financial Transaction Reporting' (1993) 4(2) *Journal of Law, Information and Science* 304.

and entities that on a professional basis, participate in the creation, administration and management of trusts and corporate vehicles'.[34] There are a range of services provided by TCSPs, including: 'acting as formation agents of legal persons' which in the offshore sector may include corporations, partnerships, foundations and trusts; acting as a director or secretary in relation to a company, a partner in relation to a partnership, or a trustee in relation to a trust; providing a registered office, business or administrative office for companies, or acting as a nominee shareholder for a third party.[35] The nature and scope of the business of TCSPs varies in that some TCSPs merely provide incorporation services to one-off clients, while others are intimately involved in the selection and creation of trust and company structure as well as the administration of the assets of their clients through family offices, including the establishment and management of bank accounts. From an AML regulatory perspective, TCSPs which provide only registration and business accommodation services are 'lower risk' than TCSPs that are involved in the management of client funds.[36]

In the case of Mossfon, the evidence suggests that it promoted and sold offshore corporate structures on a massive scale. The type of services provided by Mossfon included the sale of shell companies and the provision of registered offices and accommodation addresses, nominee directors and nominee shareholders. It is arguable that Mossfon was not a high risk TCSP in that it sold shell companies to 'respectable' intermediaries, such as banks and professional firms, and that for the most part Mossfon did not take an active role in the management of clients' assets. However, the nature of the Panama Papers revelations may suggest that larger TCSPs pose a higher AML risk even if they do not specifically manage the assets of the clients or end-clients. It is time to reconsider whether the risk rating of TCSPs should take into account the number of clients and geographical spread of its clients. In my opinion, large TCSPs should be treated as entailing higher AML risk unless it can be shown that their compliance enforcement is sufficient to address the scale of their activities.

Under the FATF Recommendations, TCSPs are required to implement customer due diligence procedures, with additional measures for higher risk clients, such as politically exposed persons, and report suspicious transactions concerning their clients. In carrying out such due diligence, there is an obligation to identify the beneficial owner of legal persons, such as companies, and legal arrangements, such as trusts. The question arises as to whether Mossfon complied with these obligations

---

34 See FATF Recommendation 12, and the glossary to the FATF Recommendations.

35 Financial Action Task Force and the Caribbean Action Task Force, *Money Laundering Using Trust and Company Service Providers* (10 October 2010) at par [21].

36 Group of International Finance Centre Supervisors, *Trust and Company Service Providers Statement of Best Practice*, at 7:<http://www.gifcs.org/images/gifcstcsstatementbestpractice.pdf> (6 September 2002).

under the global standards and Panamanian law. In a statement issued not long after the Panama Papers were published Mossfon stated:[37]

> we have always complied with international protocols ... to assure as (sic) is reasonably possible, that the companies we incorporate are not being used for tax evasion, money laundering, terrorist finance or other illicit purposes. We conduct thorough due diligence on all new and prospective clients that often exceeds in stringency the existing rules and standards to which we and others are bound. Many of our clients come through established and reputable law firms and financial institutions across the world, including the major correspondent banks, which are also bound by international 'know your client' (KYC) protocols and their own domestic regulations and laws. We are not involved in managing our clients' companies. Excluding the professional fees we earn, we do not take possession or custody of clients' money, or have anything to do with any of the direct financial aspects related to operating their businesses.

There are a series of issues arising from Mossfon's defence of its conduct. Firstly, there is overwhelming evidence as revealed by the journalistic stories accompanying the Panama Papers that Mossfon's end-clients engaged in a wide range of alleged financial crimes, including money laundering, corruption, tax evasion and sanctions violations. There is no explanation as to how this was possible unless Mossfon did not carry out adequate due diligence, or that Mossfon merely ignored the risks of known end-clients, for example, politically exposed clients who were hiding behind offshore corporate structures. The failure of Mossfon to comply with its AML compliance obligations is illustrated by a spreadsheet authored by one of its employees, which showed that of the 14,086 companies registered in Seychelles, Mossfon had obtained beneficial ownership information on only 204 companies.[38] Unfortunately, we do not know whether Mossfon tried to solve this problem or whether it was an ongoing issue when the Panama Papers were published.

Secondly, according to Mossfon more than 90 per cent of its clients were professional clients who were subject to regulation in their home jurisdiction. The question arises as to what extent can Mossfon rely on the due diligence carried out by its clients on their own clients in order to comply with its money laundering obligations? Mossfon should not have assumed that all of its professional clients are subject to comprehensive AML laws in their home jurisdiction. It was also apparent that Mossfon's sales personnel were aware that many of their end-clients were seeking secrecy structures to conceal income from tax authorities,[39] and yet they did not take

---

37 *Mossack Fonseca's response to the Panama Papers, decoded* (3 April 2016): <https://qz.com/654080/mossack-fonsecas-defense-of-its-business-in-the-offshore-financial-industry-decoded/>.

38 Bastian Obermayer and Frederik Obermaier, above n1 at 110.

39 Id at 149.

any additional measures to deal with these risks.

Thirdly, it is important to note that Mossfon was not just a TCSP but also a law firm which made it attractive to clients who may be assisting criminals and tax evaders. Here there is a relationship between the supply of corporate vehicles and the regulation of TCSPs and the professions under AML laws. A key consideration is that sophisticated criminals will invariably seek professional expert advice as to the most suitable corporate vehicle(s) and jurisdiction(s) to allow them to conceal their illicit conduct and launder illicit gains.[40] The knowledge, skill set and reputation of the legal profession, especially in the selection and management of corporate structures, coupled with the doctrine of legal professional privilege, make lawyers attractive from the perspective of organised crime.[41] Although, there are relatively few reported cases of legal professionals deliberately and wittingly facilitating financial crimes, there is a widespread perception within law enforcement and intelligence agencies that lawyers allow themselves to be used for money laundering.[42] Although the FATF Recommendations require that AML obligations should be extended beyond financial institutions to TCSPs and the legal profession, there is a poor record of implementation, with lawyers in countries such as the United States and Australia not being subject to AML oversight.

Offshore Jurisdictions and the Panama Papers

There is no precise definition of an offshore financial centre (OFC), just as there is no clear definition of a tax haven. In 2013 the International Monetary Fund (IMF) for the purpose of its statistical analysis defined an OFC as a country or jurisdiction which has 'financial institutions that deal primarily with non-residents and/or in a foreign currency on a scale out of proportion to the size of the host economy'.[43] This neutral definition emphasised that the largest proportion of financial sector activity of an OFC is offshore, in that the 'counterparties of the majority of financial institutions liabilities and assets are non-residents'.[44] However, from a law enforcement or regulatory perspective, OFCs have traditionally been associated with the following characteristics: '(i) the primary orientation of business toward non-residents; (ii) the favorable regulatory environment (low supervisory requirements

---

40 See Financial Action Task Force and the Caribbean Action Task Force, above n35 at 8.

41 See David Chaikin, 'Financial Crime Risks and the Professions', chapter 1 in David Chaikin (ed), *Financial Crime Risks, Globalisation and the Professions* (Australian Scholarly Publishing, 2013) at 1–15.

42 Id at xi.

43 International Monetary Fund, *External Debt Statistics: Guide for Compilers and Users – Appendix III, Glossary*, 2003, Washington DC.

44 International Monetary Fund, *Offshore Financial Centres: Background Paper* (23 June 2000).

and minimal information disclosure) and; (iii) the low-or zero-taxation schemes'.[45] The reference to low levels of information disclosure is perhaps a euphemism for 'banking secrecy and anonymity'.[46]

According to the Panama Papers website, Mossfon registered trusts and companies in 21 countries, including major, mid-sized and small OFCs and international financial centres. The website details the top ten jurisdictions in terms of number of incorporated entities arising from the Panama Papers: 1) British Virgin Island (113,648); 2) Panama (48,360); 3) Bahamas (15,315); 4) Seychelles (15,182); 5) Niue (9,611); 6) Samoa (5307); 7) British Anguilla (3,253); 8) Nevada, United States (1,260); 9) Hong Kong SAR (452); and 10) United Kingdom (148).

This website shows how corporate vehicles in onshore jurisdictions, such as the United States and the UK, are just as attractive as offshore corporate vehicles. The small Pacific island jurisdictions of Niue and Samoa rank highly, while a search of the Panama Papers database also discloses corporate entities in other countries in the Asia/Pacific region, namely Brunei, Cook Islands, Labuan (Malaysia), Marshall Islands, New Zealand, The People's Republic of China, Singapore and Thailand. As discussed above, there are no Australian companies listed in the website, while 47 New Zealand companies have been pinpointed in the Panama Papers.

According to one commentator,[47] the jurisdictions identified in the Panama Papers as the most popular are not necessarily those that have the highest ratings of financial secrecy.[48] However, care must be taken in interpreting the country statistics from the Panama Papers because we do not know the specific reasons why a particular country was selected as the jurisdiction of incorporation, and whether this was a result of advice from Mossfon or was a direct request of its clients. The relative importance of jurisdictions used by Mossfon must take into account the fact that the statistics are from only one of the world's leading TCSPs. These statistics are not surprising in that the British Virgin Islands is the world's largest market for the establishment of International Business Companies, especially for Chinese and Hong Kong citizens. That Panama is the second most popular jurisdiction would seem to follow from the fact that Mossfon is headquartered in Panama.

The Panama Papers has raised the question whether intergovernmental bodies, such as the FATF and the OECD, should reconsider its 'blacklist' of OFCs. Although the FATF does not have a blacklist per se, it does issue a list of uncooperative

---

45 Ahmed Zo, *Concept of Offshore Financial Centres: In Search of an Operational Definition*, IMF Working Paper, WP/07/87, April 2007 at 4.

46 International Monetary Fund, above n44.

47 Uri Friedman, 'The Geography of Offshore Secrecy', *The Atlantic*): <http://www.theatlantic.com/international/archive/2016/04/panama-papers-tax-havens-world/477042/> (9 April 2006).

48 See Tax Justice Network, *Financial Secrecy Index*: <http://www.financialsecrecyindex.com/introduction/fsi-2015-results>.

jurisdictions, whose AML laws and policies are deficient. However, it is highly ironic that just prior to the publication of the Panama Papers in April 2016, the FATF, in February 2016, removed Panama from its grey list; only Iran and North Korea are identified as high AML risk countries that should be subject to counter-measures. The OECD also has a list of non-cooperative tax havens, that is, jurisdictions which do not cooperate in combatting tax evasion, but this list has been whittled down so that by June 2017, there was only one country on the list, the small country of Trinidad and Tobago in the Caribbean.[49]

This is a vexed policy issue as to whether intergovernmental organisations should impose sanctions or counter-measures on OFCs (usually small developing countries) which have deficiencies in their laws, policies and enforcement in relation to crimes such as money laundering or tax evasion. It has been suggested that trade tariffs should be imposed on those OFCs which do not provide effect co-operation, and that the tariffs should be the equivalent of the 'recovery of costs of financial secrecy'.[50] The problem with this approach is that it discriminates against the weaker OFCs, while the wealthy international financial centres, such as London or New York, escape any penalty for evading or avoiding responsibility for facilitating international financial crime.

Conclusions

The Panama Papers have shone a light on the massive offshore TCSP industry which is an essential cog in international finance and money laundering. From a law enforcement perspective, the Panama Papers has resulted in a closing of the information deficit gap which arises because domestic authorities are unaware that a person has funds in an offshore jurisdiction. The Panama Papers has proved to be valuable by disclosing the secret beneficial ownership and control structures used by criminals and tax evaders. What is interesting is that in a number of cases the intermediaries disclosed to Mossfon the true beneficial owner or controller of the corporate structures, thereby enabling the journalists at the ICIJ to investigate the illicit activities of the end-clients. It seems that the end-clients believed that their secrets were safe with the intermediaries. In the future, it is likely that criminals and tax evaders will take additional measures to ensure that their corporate structures are more secret, thereby resulting in a new arms race between those who seek secrecy and those who wish to uncover such secrets.

---

49 See Alex Cobhham, 'Empty OECD 'tax haven' blacklist undermines progress', *Tax Justice Network* (28 June 2017).

50 Gabriel Zucman, *The Hidden Wealth of Nations: The Scourge of Tax Havens* (University of Chicago Press 2016) at 81–2.

Chapter 10

Money Laundering, Professionals, Companies and Trusts

Dr Gordon Hook and Nick McTaggart

As the United Nations Office on Drugs and Crime (UNODC) has stated '[t]he term economic and financial crime … comprises a broad range of illegal activities, including fraud, tax evasion and money-laundering. The category of 'economic crime' is hard to define and its exact conceptualisation remains a challenge … complicated by rapid advances in technology, which provide new opportunities for such crimes.'[1]

This chapter will look at the phenomenon of money laundering as a sub-set of economic or financial crime and the activities associated with it including the use of professionals and corporate structures in the laundering process. The first half of this chapter is an outline of some of the main areas of interest and the second half is a question and answer exchange between the authors.

Background

According to a 2009 report of the UNODC, the best estimate for the amount of criminal proceeds available for laundering in the financial system is equivalent to 2.7 per cent of global GDP or US$1.6 trillion.[2] The single largest amount comes from illicit drugs which account for approximately 20 per cent of all global criminal proceeds.[3] Estimating the volume of money laundering in Australia is not an easy task. However, in 2009 the Australian Institute of Criminology estimated that $4.5 billion of criminal proceeds are laundered in Australia every year.[4] Recent large scale drug seizures, in 2016 and 2017, and the rising tide of fraud (including digital credit card theft and other cyber-crimes) may very well mean that the scale of money laundering in Australia is much higher than estimated. According to a Price Waterhouse Cooper (Australia) report in 2016:

1 United Nations Office on Drugs and Crime (2005), 'Economic And Financial Crimes: Challenges To Sustainable Development': <http://www.unis.unvienna.org/pd-f/05-82108_E_5_pr_SFS.pdf>.

2 UNODC (2009) 'Estimating Illicit Financial Flows Resulting From Drug Trafficking And Other Transnational Organized Crimes': <http://www.unodc.org/documents/data-and-analysis/Studies/Illicit_financial_flows_2011_web.pdf>.

3 Id at 7.

4 Australian Institute of Criminology (2009): <http://www.aic.gov.au/crime_types/transnational/moneylaundering.html>.

Money laundering was experienced by Australian respondents at a significantly higher rate than the global average over the last 24 months (26 per cent and 11 per cent respectively) and continues to increase compared to the previous two surveys (approximately 16 per cent in 2012 and 18 per cent in 2014).[5]

This comment was supported by AUSTRAC, Australia's anti-money laundering regulator, when it was reported in the same year that, 'Financial crime is on the rise in Australia, with the country's senior money-laundering officials saying they've [sic] witnessed a dramatic increase in fraudulent transactions.'[6]

What is Money Laundering?

The term 'proceeds of crime' is defined in Australian law to mean any money or property that is wholly or partially derived or realised (directly or indirectly) from the commission of an offence.[7] Money laundering can be described simply as dealing with the proceeds of crime in ways that make those proceeds appear to have come from legitimate sources.[8] All one can ever achieve in a money-laundering cycle is the 'appearance' of legitimacy, never 'actual' legitimacy. As we will see below, the use of companies, trusts and professionals in the money-laundering process can go a long way to facilitating this appearance. Traditionally, the money-laundering process has been analysed in simple terms involving the following steps:[9]

1. 'placement' of proceeds of crime in the financial system (e.g. deposit of illicit funds directly in a bank account or a lawyer's trust account);
2. 'layering' or engaging in a series of transactions to distance the criminal proceeds from the original crime (e.g. multiple transfers of those funds to other bank accounts, including off-shore accounts, withdrawal of funds then re-depositing in another person's name);
3. 'integration' in which the funds re-enter the legitimate economy (e.g. for instance, by withdrawing the funds and purchasing a home or business).

However, as will be discussed later, some money-laundering schemes involving corporate entities and cross-border transactions are more complex than this simple framework and, in any event, Division 400 of the *Criminal Code Act* 1995 (Cth)

---

5 Price Waterhouse Cooper (2106), *Global Economic Crime Survey 2016 / Australian Report*, at 10: <http://www.pwc.com.au/consulting/assets/global-economic-crime/global-economic-crime-survey-2016-australian-report.pdf>.

6 <http://www.smh.com.au/business/financial-crime-on-the-rise-austrac-20160622-gppavx.html>.

7 Sub-division 400.1 of the *Criminal Code Act* 1995 (Cth).

8 See AUSTRAC (2011), *Money Laundering in Australia 2011* at: http://www.austrac.gov.au/sites/default/files/documents/money_laundering_in_australia_2011.pdf>.

9 See John Cassara, *Hide and Seek: Intelligence, Law Enforcement, and the Stalled War on Terrorist Finance* (Dulles, Virginia: Potomac Books, Inc., 2006); FATF (2017), *How is Money Laundered?*:<http://www.fatf-gafi.org/faq/moneylaundering/>.

categorises money laundering as including mere receipt, possession, or concealment of criminal proceeds. Hence, the mere possession of drug sale proceeds or their concealment, including stuffing them in a mattress, without any transactional 'layering' can amount to a money-laundering offence.[10]

There are two types of money-laundering activities:

1. self-laundering; and
2. third-party laundering.

Self-laundering is a term used to describe the activity of laundering criminal proceeds by the criminal who committed the underlying predicate crime. Those who engage in self-laundering retain direct responsibility for, and control of, the movement of the proceeds of crime in the attempt to make those proceeds appear legitimate. The advantage of self-laundering is that it ensures that information about the various transactions involved in the money-laundering process is restricted to the person laundering the proceeds or to small number of persons, such as a criminal group or enterprise. However, it is unlikely that self-laundering will ever again take on the audacious dimensions that were seen over 30 years ago, well before the international standards against money laundering were set by the Financial Action Task Force (FATF). In a 1982 United States case, over US$242 million in cash was deposited at one bank over the course of a few months by drug dealers, smelling of 'dope', carrying paper bags and suitcases full of cash for tellers to count.[11] With cash transaction reporting thresholds designed to detect and ultimately prevent this type of activity, criminals use more sophisticated methods to get their criminal proceeds into financial institutions, including the use of companies, trusts and lawyers.

Third-party laundering refers to the laundering of criminal proceeds by a person unconnected with the predicate crime.[12] Often the third party is a family member or

---

10 Some cases in Australia have limited the ability to charge both for the predicate offence and for self-laundering. See for instance: *Nahlous v R* (2010) 201 ACrimR 150; *Thorn v R* (2010) 198 ACrimR 135; *Schembri v R* (2010) 28 ATR 159).

11 *United States v. $4,255,625.39*, 551 F Supp 314 (S.D. Fla. 1982). Similar cases were reported in Canada at about the same time when members of the Caruana-Cuntrera mafia family placed bags of cash in pick-up trucks, backed the trucks up to a bank's front door and threw the bags to the bank staff inside to empty, count and deposit. Once deposited, the money was quickly wire-transferred to offshore accounts. See Nicaso and Lamothe, *Bloodlines: Rise and Fall of Mafia's Royal Family* (Toronto: Harper Collins 2000).

12 See United Nations Convention against Transnational Organised Crime Article 6(1) (e) and FATF Assessment Methodology Recommendation 3.5: <https://www.unodc.org/documents/middleeastandnorthafrica/organised-crime/UNITED_NATIONS_CONVEN-TION_AGAINST_TRANSNATIONAL_ORGANIZED_CRIME_AND_THE_PRO-TOCOLS_THERETO.pdf>; and <http://www.fatf-gafi.org/media/fatf/documents/methodology/FATF per cent20Methodology per cent2022 per cent20Feb per cent202013.pdf>.

friend engaged for that purpose but it may also include professionals such as lawyers, accountants and other professionals who have expertise in forming and managing company structures. These persons are simply responsible for the movement of the criminal proceeds through the various stages outlined above. Ironically, many criminals who commit the predicate crime generating the illegal proceeds believe that if they engage the services of someone, who was not a party to that crime to undertake the transactions needed to generate a veneer of legitimacy for the illicit money, that they reduce their risk of being charged with the offence of money laundering. However, engaging the third-party launderer and transferring the funds to that person is by definition money laundering regardless of what the third party does with those funds. And since Australian criminal law does not require that the third party be convicted of the predicate crime,[13] the third party also commits a laundering offence by simply receiving those funds.

Using Professionals and Corporate Structures

In increasing numbers, criminals use companies, trusts and the professionals, who establish those structures, to launder the proceeds of their crime. An AUSTRAC report in 2015 highlighted the areas of service in which lawyers, in particular, could be exploited for money laundering.[14] Shortly thereafter, in early 2016, the data disclosed in the Panama Paper revelations, illustrated the extent to which lawyers, offering company formation services, not only could be but clearly were used in money-laundering schemes. In their recent book, Bastian Obermayer and Frederick Obermaier,[15] the journalists who broke the story of the Panama Papers, outlined how the law firm of Mossack Fonseca (Mossack), based in Panama, used a web of agents around the globe to establish companies on their behalf for the purpose of hiding and moving illicit funds. Criminals would engage a lawyer in their own jurisdiction, who in turn would contact the offices of Mossack and request the sale of a company, usually in an off-shore tax haven. Off-shore tax havens have strict banking and corporate secrecy laws which shield the identity of persons involved in company formation and management and therefore hamper international cooperation with law enforcement authorities.[16] Mossack would, in turn, engage one of its agents (usually another law firm) in the off-shore jurisdiction

---

13 Section 400.13 *Criminal Code Act* 1995 (Australia).

14 AUSTRAC, *Money Laundering Through Legal Practitioners* (2015): <http://www.austrac.gov.au/sites/default/files/sa-brief-legal-practitioners.pdf>.

15 Bastian Obermayer and Frederick Obermaier, *The Panama Papers: Breaking the Story of How the Rich and Powerful Hide Their Money* (London: One World Publications Limited, 2017).

16 See David Chaikin (ed.) *Money Laundering, Tax Evasion and Tax Havens* (Sydney: Australian Scholarly Publishing Pty Ltd, 2009) in particular Chapter 7 entitled *Tax Havens: An Australian Perspective*.

(e.g. British Virgin Islands, Bermuda, Samoa, Delaware etc.) who would form the company, transmit its proper documents to Mossack who would then do the same to the original law firm. That firm would then sell the company to the criminal clients who first requested it. Mossack's clients were the original law firm (or in some cases a financial institution) and not the final user of the company entity. Once received, the companies themselves would engage agents to act as company directors and could be utilized to open bank accounts or purchase assets. Together with the secrecy provisions prohibiting disclosure of information about the company in the country where the company was formed, and the use of agents to act in company positions such as secretary or director, criminals could engage in these laundering transactions with virtual anonymity.

In a recent investigation into shell companies used to evade tax in Australia, it was determined that shell companies were used to 'legitimise' false expenses for companies in Australia in order to reduce their income tax. An accountant based in Vanuatu registered shell companies in a number of countries including New Zealand, the United Kingdom, Ireland, the United States and Vanuatu. The accountant used the certificates of incorporation of the shell companies to establish up 150 foreign currency accounts in New Zealand. Over a period of 10 years the accounts were used to evade an estimated $100 million of tax by Australian citizens. Approximately $30 million dollars was seized in bank accounts held by the shell companies.[17]

Apart from the use of legal professionals for establishing corporate structures criminals may also use legal professionals wittingly or unwittingly to launder their criminal proceeds. A particular vulnerability is associated with lawyers' client or trust accounts. With respect to the latter criminals may request that their funds be deposited into a lawyer's trust account and either held there until needed or transferred to another account. In either case the criminal's name is not disclosed to the bank and is subject to legal professional privilege. An example of this type of activity is reported in a recent New Zealand Financial Intelligence Unit report.[18] During a police operation called 'Operation Rock' two drug dealers laundered $400,000 in cash through a lawyer's trust account. The lawyer did not undertake any due diligence checks on his clients nor did he report any suspicious transactions involving the receipt of the cash. The bank in which the lawyer's trust account was held did, however, submit suspicious transaction reports when the lawyer deposited $100,000 on four occasions. The offenders had instructed the lawyer to deposit the funds into an account in the name of a company registered in Gibraltar. This company was a shell company that 'lent' one of the offenders the $400,000 in order

---

17 Financial Intelligence Unit (New Zealand Police) 2014, *Abuse of Shell Companies* at 11: <http://www.police.govt.nz/advice/businesses-and-organisations/fiu/news-and-documents>.

18 Financial Intelligence Unit (New Zealand Police) 2014, *Money Laundering and Terrorist Through Professional Client Accounts* at 8: <http://www.police.govt.nz/sites/default/files/pub-lications/fiu-quarterly-typology-report-q3-2013-2014.pdf>.

to purchase a property in Auckland. Another lawyer was engaged by the offender to facilitate this 'loan' and the purchase of the house in the offender's name. The funds for the purchase of the property therefore looked legitimate (a loan from a company). Effectively, two lawyers from different law firms had been involved in the money-laundering process.

Some law societies prohibit the use of lawyers' accounts for this purpose. While other law societies have strict rules in relation to the acceptance of cash by lawyers from their clients.[19]

Question and Answer Exchange:

Gordon Hook: Nick, you were a law enforcement officer with the Australian Federal Police for over 38 years with significant experience in the investigation of financial crime including money laundering. Is money laundering a profitable exercise for criminals?

Nick McTaggart: I would not consider the traditional money-laundering methodologies used by self-launderers to be profitable in the same context as other forms of economic or financial crime, such as market manipulation or fraud. However, criminals do 'profit' in a sense from successful money-laundering activity even if it involves a monetary loss, because the purpose of money laundering is to make criminal proceeds appear to be legitimate funds. A simple but good example of a traditional form of self-laundering involves the purchase of motor vehicles with the proceeds of drug sales, and then on-selling of those vehicles for cash, even if it involves a loss, to make the drug sale proceeds appear to be the proceeds of legitimate car sales. For criminals, the direct and calculable loss in funds from the transaction is considered simply the cost of doing business. At the same time, the transactions are considered 'profitable' because of the 'gain' achieved in making the illicit proceeds appear legitimate.

When considering professional third-party money-laundering syndicates, the answer to your question is definitely yes. For (predicate) criminals, a relationship with a professional third-party money-laundering syndicate will, over time, see reductions in the commissions they pay to those professionals and therefore, in turn, more profit in their pockets. In 2015, I was the co-author of a typologies report for the FATF and the APG which focused on the vulnerabilities of the gold market to money laundering. The paper provides an example of how fees or commissions paid to third-party launderers by criminals may decline once a relationship is

19 For example the Federation of Law Societies of Canada developed a model rule that pro-hibits lawyers from receiving any cash exceeding $ 7 500 for any one transaction. See *Model Rule on Cash Transactions* (2004), paragraph 1: <http://flsc.ca/wp-content/uploads/2014/10/terror1.pdf>.

established.[20] In early 2014, the French police uncovered an international money-laundering network that laundered the proceeds of the sale of cannabis in Paris. Moroccan dealers smuggled hash to France and sold it at street level in a six-month period raising over 30 million euros. An Indian national, on behalf of an organised syndicate, collected the proceeds, deposited those proceeds into different accounts of companies associated with a gold trader and then purchased gold and jewellery with those proceeds in the various bank accounts. The syndicate's profit was based upon the conversion and resale of gold. The syndicate was able to sell gold for a competitive market price and make a profit. The gold in question was purchased at 31 euros per gram in Belgium and resold for 36.32 euros per gram in Dubai. The gold trader received a fee of 325 euros per kilogram which equated to a profit of 5,000 euros per kilogram for the syndicate. This system was so profitable that the syndicate waived its usual money-laundering commission of 2.25 per cent to the (predicate) criminal and worked entirely for the profit generated.

Gordon Hook: In your opinion how adept are criminals at using companies and trusts to launder criminal proceeds?

Nick McTaggart: Since Australia enacted money-laundering and terrorist-financing laws, including forfeiture and seizure laws to recover criminal proceeds, criminals have become more aware of the value of utilising corporate structures to hide, move and profit from their criminal activity. Companies are fairly easy to form in Australia and because they are commonly used in business transactions, and at the same time allow the names of owners and managers to be shielded from disclosure to financial institutions when opening accounts, they are attractive to criminal groups.

In addition, companies allow criminal groups to 'fracture' their money-laundering activity across different business structures and different countries. For instance, the use of multiple companies to move money can assist in obscuring the money trail, especially where one or more of those companies is a foreign company. On that point, criminal groups tend to take advantage of so-called 'tax havens' and 'off-shore' jurisdictions which have company and trust secrecy laws. Those laws further complicate the ability of law enforcement agencies not only to identify the criminals at work in those entities, but also to trace and seize the criminal proceeds.

When it comes to trusts, it is a bit more complex; therein lies the attraction for criminals. Trusts are more complicated to set up than companies, generally not as well understood by the average person including some financial institutions, and there are no registration requirements as a pre-condition to a trust's legal status. Moreover, under Australian law there is no requirement that trustees obtain and hold

---

20 B. Kumar and N. McTaggart, *Money Laundering and Terrorist Financing Risks and Vulnerabilities Associated with Gold* (2015) at: <http://www.apgml.org/methods-and-trends/documents/default.aspx>.

adequate, accurate and current information on the identity of the principal parties to a trust (settlors, trustees, and beneficiaries) including anyone who may exercise ultimate control over a trust. This makes a law enforcement money-laundering investigation involving a trust more difficult. Getting behind a trust structure to determine who the criminals are can be next to impossible. As one reporter recently said 'Transparency campaigners say the veil of secrecy around trusts in Australia is shielding tax rip-offs, corruption, money laundering, even terrorism.'[21] In *CDPP v. Hart*[22], a Queensland accountant engaged in systematic tax fraud, by running a number of tax avoidance schemes involving his clients. He set up a complex trusts with family members to launder the proceeds of crime and to hold assets, partially purchased with the proceeds of tax evasion.

Criminals have also come to recognise that not only can they can move their illicit money through corporate structures and trusts but by labelling some of the establishment costs to set up a network of companies and trusts as 'expenses', they also commit other and profitable economic crimes.

Gordon Hook: Nick do you know of any cases in which lawyers have themselves been prosecuted and found guilty of money laundering?

Nick McTaggart: Lawyers are not immune from investigation and prosecution for money laundering on behalf of the clients. There was a case reported this year (2017) in which a lawyer used criminal proceeds provided by his client to purchase real estate for that client as part of a laundering transaction.[23] The court found that the lawyer was aware that the funds were the proceeds of crime and that in acting for the client in the transactions he was guilty of money laundering. Other recent cases against lawyers have involved structuring criminal proceeds, provided by criminals to their lawyers, to defeat the requirements of the reporting cash transactions requirements.[24]

I have been in quite a few cases myself. During some of my investigations associated

---

21 Royce Millar and Ben Schneiders, 'Whatever you do, don't mention the trusts', *Sydney Morning Herald*: <http://www.smh.com.au/national/whatever-you-do-dont-mention-the-trusts-20170406-gvf2pk.html>.

22 *DPP v Hart* [2004] QDC 121.

23 'Disgraced lawyer John Anile guilty of money laundering', *Herald Sun* (22 June 2017): <http://www.heraldsun.com.au/news/law-order/disgraced-lawyer-john-anile-guilty-of-money-laundering/news-story/fc275cb60a58a64e043be8945f4c4628>; Also see: *The Age* (30 June 2017), 'Laundering lawyer John Anile sentenced to three years jail': <http://www.theage.com.au/victoria/laundering-lawyer-john-anile-sentenced-to-three-years-jail-20170630-gx1y0t.html>

24 'Lawyers charged with money-laundering proceeds of crime', *Brisbane Times* (2015): <http://www.brisbanetimes.com.au/queensland/lawyers-charged-with-moneylaundering-proceeds-of-crime-20150112-12mft3.html>.

with Project Wickenby[25], a registered accountant based in Vanuatu promoted a scheme to several small businesses in Australia through local accountants. The scheme was promoted as a tax-minimisation scheme. However, during negotiations between the parties they became aware that tax evasion could also be committed with little risk of identification by Australian revenue authorities. The scheme relied on a 'discretionary trust'[26] that was to receive funds from the subject small business. These funds included both legitimate profit from the business and additional revenue generated though the illegal claim of expenses incurred by that business undertaking normal business activity. A common example of these illegal expense claims was the supply of business reports purported to be provided to the business to help them expand. The cost of compilation of these reports and the contents of the reports were a sham with numerous examples where reports alleged to have cost many thousands of dollars, were in fact just a compilation of random pages drawn from internet content which often had nothing to do with the businesses in question.

The police investigation identified a very complex web of company and trust structures operating through several jurisdictions to help disguise criminal activity including tax evasion, fraud and money laundering. Instrumental in selling the scheme to the business owners in relation to the fund-ownership anonymity, was the ruse that the business would always have access to the funds in question. In truth the business owners had in fact signed away their legal rights and no longer had legal ownership or control over the amount that was the subject of the criminal activity.

During the period prior to interdiction, the period I will refer to as the 'harmony period', the scheme worked well for all parties concerned, even though the business owners had signed over, at law, all the funds in the scheme (which amounted to millions of dollars) by virtue of the existence of the discretionary trust. The arrangement was the Vanuatu based accountant would 'gift' to the relevant participants funds from the trust. These gifts were not subject to tax. After interdiction, the participants quickly found out that, at law, the trustee of the trust, which in this case was the Vanuatu accountant, had total discretion over the distribution of all the funds. Further, the Vanuatu accountant subsequently determined that he would need the funds in the trust to pursue his legal defence.

---

25 Project Wickenby was commenced in 2006 to protect the integrity of Australia's financial and regulatory systems by preventing people from promoting or participating in the abuse of off-shore secrecy arrangements: <https://www.ato.gov.au/General/The-fight-against-tax-crime/Our-focus/Project-Wickenby-task-force/> (24 July 2017).

26 In a discretionary trust (or family trust) the beneficiaries do not have a fixed entitlement or interest in the trust funds. The trustee has the discretion to determine which of the beneficiaries is to receive the capital and income of the trust and how much each beneficiary is to receive. The trustee does not have complete discretion. The trustee can only distribute to beneficiaries within a nominated class as set out in the terms of the trust deed. See: <http://www.findlaw.com.au/articles/4606/what-is-a-discretionary-trust-and-what-are-the-ben.aspx>.

The irony of this scheme is, of course, that the participants discovered that their activity attempted to avoid the payment of 30 per cent of the funds contributed to the trust to Australian revenue authorities and that the owner of the scheme had ownership and discretion over 100 per cent of the funds. These participants approached investigators for assistance to recover the 70 per cent of contributions and were very dejected when they were told there was nothing that could be done at law and that their participation in the scheme was significantly more punishing than if they had simply paid the tax owing in the first instance. The footnote to this case study is that all the participants in question had significantly profitable businesses and it was only greed on their part that had brought about their demise.

Gordon Hook: What challenges need to be addressed to see more successes in the investigation and disruption of economic crime using corporate structures and trusts?

Nick McTaggart: With respect to companies there are some provisions in the law, including convictions for offences, which prohibit criminals from owning and managing companies but the range of those offences is very limited. Even with respect to those limited offences there is a lack of oversight to enforce those prohibitions including oversight of whether someone is acting on behalf of someone else who has been convicted of a criminal offence. The laws could be tightened up in that regard to ensure that criminals of any sort are barred from owning and operating companies.

Moreover, under the current law, there are limited disclosure requirements of the 'beneficial owners' of companies. When investigating financial crimes involving companies it is very often difficult for law enforcement authorities to trace who actually owns a company that is suspected of being involved in a money laundering scheme. The corporate registry in ASIC is only a starting point and the company's own members' (shareholders') register is often unhelpful. That register may disclose that the shareholders are other companies. When law enforcement authorities investigate those other companies, they may themselves be owned by more companies and so on. If one or more of those companies is owned by a company incorporated in a foreign jurisdiction then the investigation is further complicated.

It is much more challenging when it comes to trusts because currently there is no registration requirement for trusts.

Gordon Hook: Australia has not yet included professionals such as accountants and lawyers within the regulatory framework of anti-money laundering and terrorist-financing supervision – the so-called 'second tranche' that we have often heard about. Do you think there is a need to include the professions within the monitoring and supervision framework?

Nick McTaggart: I believe that lawmakers should level the playing field between financial institutions which are included within Australia's supervision framework and professionals that are gatekeepers to those institutions. New Zealand is moving ahead of Australia in this regard with proposed legislation, to include lawyers and accountants, to be enacted by the end of this year (2017), and many other like-minded countries (such as the United Kingdom) already include the professions within their supervision framework. The longer Australia lags behind in this area and while other countries are plugging the gaps the more Australia will be seen as an easy target to exploit. And this will likely have reputational issues for Australia which may affect what we in Australia like to think of as a solid financial and regulatory system with effective law enforcement authorities.

Nick McTaggart: I would like to ask the last question of you, Gordon. As Executive Secretary of the Asia/Pacific Group on Money Laundering what, if anything, is happening in the FATF to address some of the concerns that have been highlighted in this discussion?

Gordon Hook: The FATF is currently looking at their standards relating to companies and trusts. They have a project underway this year (2017) in which they are examining the vulnerabilities linked to companies and trusts and what to do about them. The report is due for completion at the end of 2017. In addition, some of the issues associated with the difference between common law countries and civil law countries regarding recommendation 25 (on trusts) are currently being examined in the FATF and it is expected that policy responses will be forthcoming very shortly. There are complex issues associated with different national legal systems when it comes to trusts.

Before I close I should point out that the FATF standards are the minimum requirements that countries need to implement in order to satisfy the international community that it has measures and programmes in place to mitigate money-laundering and terrorist-financing risks. Countries themselves can implement measures that go beyond the FATF standards. And some countries have done that. For instance, in 2016 the United Kingdom implemented measures in relation to companies that require disclosure of beneficial ownership well beyond the FATF standards, and next year (2018) they will be implementing similar measures for trusts (including registration requirements).

Contributors

David Bennett

David Bennett AC QC has been a Queen's Counsel since 1979. He was made an officer in the order of Australia in 2000 and was made a Companion in the General Division of the Order of Australia in 2008. He completed his LLB at Sydney University with first class honours in 1964, his LLM at Harvard in 1965 and his SJD at Harvard in 1970.

He has presided over many influential bodies including the Australian Bar Association; the Medico Legal Society of NSW; the Association of Barrister Arbitrators and Mediators; the Australian Academy of Forensic Sciences, and contributed to the International Commission of Jurists, Australian Section and NSW Section; the Australian delegation of the Hague Conference on Private International law, Judgments and Choice of Court conventions; the International Academy of Estate and Trust Law: South Pacific Region; the International Legal Services Advisory Council and the Takeovers Panel. David was Solicitor-General of Australia from 1998–2008.

David Chaikin

Dr David Chaikin is the Chair of the Discipline of Business Law and an Associate Professor at the University of Sydney's School of Business. David teaches and researches in Banking and Finance Law, International Financial Crime and the Law of Asset Protection. David has been a practising lawyer for more than 30 years and previously held the position of Senior Assistant Secretary in the Australian Attorney-General's Department, and Senior Legal Officer of the London-based diplomatic body, the Commonwealth Secretariat. David is co-editor and/or co-author of *Digital Disruption: Impact on Business Models, Financial Crime and Regulation* (2016); *Financial Crime Risks, Globalisation and the Professions* (2013); *Money Laundering, Tax Evasion & Tax Havens* (2009); *Corruption and Money Laundering: A Symbiotic Relationship* (2009). He has a doctorate of law from Cambridge University, a Masters of Law from Yale Law School, and double degrees in Law and Commerce (Accounting, Finance & Systems) from the University of New South Wales.

Derwent Coshott

Derwent Coshott has a BA (UNSW), JD (Syd), GradDipLegalPrac (ColLaw), LLM (Syd). Derwent is a PhD candidate at the University of Sydney. His research interests centre on the laws of trusts and property. Derwent's PhD thesis is entitled 'The Legal and Economic Development of the Express Trust: Advancing a Conceptual Model for the Development and Reform of the Express Trust'. Derwent is also a co-author of the upcoming 6th edition of 'Sale of Land in NSW: Commentary and Materials'.

He regularly lectures for both the University of Sydney Business School and the Sydney Law School.

Gordon Hook

Dr Gordon Hook is the Executive Secretary of the Asia/Pacific Group on Money Laundering (APG), a multi-lateral organisation of 41 countries and jurisdictions in the Asia-Pacific region responsible for the implementation of the international standards against money laundering and terrorist financing. Prior to his current position he practised law as a partner in a Winnipeg, Canada law firm in the 1980s and 1990s. He then served in the Royal New Zealand Navy (RNZN) as a senior legal officer which included a five month tour in the Persian Gulf from November 2002 to April 2003 as the naval task force legal advisor during US-led Operation Enduring Freedom. After serving in the RNZN he joined the New Zealand Ministry of Justice as the Manager of Criminal and International Law where he led a team responsible for New Zealand's AML/CFT reform programme. Gordon Hook holds a BA and MA from the University of Manitoba in Canada; an LLB from Dalhousie University in Canada; and a PhD (Law) from Victoria University of Wellington in New Zealand. He is a Barrister and Solicitor of the Manitoba Queen's Bench and of the High Court of New Zealand.

Carla Hoorweg

Carla Hoorweg is the Senior Policy Manager for Investment and Technology & Innovation at the Financial Services Council. Carla has over 17 years' experience in the financial services industry and has worked in product and legal roles as well as serving as a ministerial advisor to the NSW state government. Carla holds a Masters of Law (Hons) and Juris Doctor from the University of Technology Sydney, an Executive MBA from the Australian Graduate School of Management, and Bachelor and Graduate degrees in Applied Psychology from the University of Canberra. Carla holds a NSW practising certificate and is a Graduate of the Australian Institute of Company Directors.

Nicholas McTaggart

Nicholas retired from the Australia Federal Police after 38 years to commence his own consultancy business Murinbin Consultancy which is part of The Murinbin Group. He has recently finished a contract consulting to AUSTRAC at the strategic level, is currently consulting to the Fijian Revenue and Custom Service and has advised other public and private sector entities. Nicholas retired as a Detective Superintendent, a position held for over 15 years. Nicholas is a very experienced subject-matter expert on anti-money laundering, economic crime and criminal asset confiscation and has been engaged in strategic planning of whole of government approaches to the problem over a number of years. He has an interest in the proliferation of new payment platforms and their risks. In the final years of his police career, Nicholas held the position of National Coordinator of the Criminal Asset Confiscation Taskforce. He was also heavily involved with linking the public and private sectors to enhance disruption of criminal activity in his areas of expertise. Nicholas was the AFP's representative on FATF and APG forums co-publishing two typology reports for those organisations as well as several other publications.

Juliette Overland

Dr Juliette Overland (LLB (Hons I) (*QUT*), PhD (*ANU*)) is an Associate Professor in the Discipline of Business Law at the University of Sydney Business School. Her research expertise is in corporate law, particularly the regulation of securities markets, insider trading, and corporate crime, and she completed her PhD thesis on the regulation of corporate liability for insider trading. Juliette is recognised as a leading authority on the regulation of insider trading and she has published widely in this area. In addition to her experience as an academic, Juliette has extensive practical experience as a corporate lawyer, having worked in leading Australian law firms and as the Australian legal counsel for a global technology company.

William Page

William Page is a dual English and New South Wales qualified lawyer who co-founded FilmDoo, which is a integrated media distribution company utilising disruptive technology to deliver the best in entertainment, cultural and language learning content. Part of the business is the FilmDoo video-on-demand platform, which is an international and independent film platform helping people to discover great films from around the world. The platform has grown to have over 500,000 visitors a month, has 2,000+ films available and has successfully raised over $700,000 to date in investment. Prior to founding FilmDoo William worked as a corporate lawyer in the UK and across the Middle East with Trowers & Hamlins, Herbert Smith Freehills and Vinson & Elkins where he worked with a number of venture capital funds and private equity funds. William is now using his legal and entrepreneurial experience to assist start-ups in overcoming challenges faced in building and launching their businesses, especially around structuring their businesses, corporate governance and in their fundraising efforts.

Zhaozhao Wu

Zhaozhao Wu is a lawyer with Teddington Legal, and a PhD candidate at the University of Sydney Business School. Her research interest includes the legal risks of online marketplaces and corporate structures of digital platforms in China, and she has published papers in China's legal and tax policies. She holds a Juris Doctor from the University of Sydney, a Bachelor of Laws from China University of Political Science and Law, and a Master of Management from the University of Melbourne. She is admitted as a lawyer in the Supreme Court of New South Wales.

Printed in Australia
Ingram Content Group Australia Pty Ltd
AUHW020925191124
402995AU00003B/76